* * * * * * *

THE AGE OF
THE SCHOLAR

* * * * * * *

©1965 National Wildlife Federation, Washington, D. C.

RED SHINER

---

harper ✦ torchbooks

*A reference-list of Harper Torchbooks, classified
by subjects, is printed at the end of this volume.*

DATE DUE

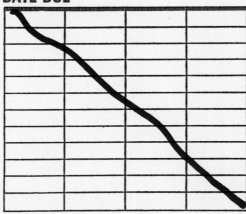

The Age of the Scholar

OBSERVATIONS ON EDUCATION IN A TROUBLED DECADE

* * * * *

NATHAN M. PUSEY

HARPER TORCHBOOKS
The Academy Library
HARPER & ROW, PUBLISHERS
NEW YORK, EVANSTON AND LONDON

* * * * * * *

FOREWORD

Looking back on ten years as a university president is sufficient cause for surprise at one's survival without reliving the birthpangs of twoscore "major" addresses and countless other moments when it was appropriate, or required, to say something suited to a special occasion. But Mr. Thomas J. Wilson, Director of the Harvard University Press, in his most persuasive North Carolinian manner has convinced me that if ever I am to make a personal selection of my papers for public view, this is the time.

To be a constant defender of his institution's good name and a willing mendicant ever ready to take the road in behalf of Alma Mater's needs are two of a university president's major responsibilities in this confusing and demanding era. I was therefore not surprised to find in re-examining my public pronouncements that a considerable portion of my work for Harvard consisted of contributions in these categories. It was relatively easy, therefore, to decide that a collection of the present sort should exclude such items, even though they may have attracted the considerable attention given my speech on college and university financing before the American Council on Education in 1958 and my discussion of the Carnegie study of the relationship between government and higher education before the same body in October 1962. Similarly I have omitted addresses chiefly of Harvard interest. The resultant collection will suggest a range of approaches to the problems of the American university in these times rather than serve as a complete documentation of an administrative decade.

One may well ask what it all proves. If there is one thing I have tried to say—and say again and again—it is that the complex and exciting organism which is a university is one of the noblest creations of the mind of man and one deserving the widest and wisest understanding. In a time of enlarging opportunity and aspiration for new nations throughout the world, the supranational network of universities, though linked by the slightest of weblike strands, is yet a powerful force for world peace. In the eagerness of the developing nations to achieve health and plenty, there are urgent pressures at work to emphasize the material benefits of the university. Such pressures characterize not only the developing nations but our own as well. It is my deep conviction, stated on more than one occasion, that true learning cannot go on in a vacuum; it is in constant interplay with society and at its center requires fundamental spiritual commitment or it is nothing. Much of my thinking and speaking has related to the compatability of materialism, secularism, and the "joy of belief" without which higher education would have no real power to affect man's highest aspirations.

If these collected essays can persuade any of the unpersuaded and reinforce the conviction of the convinced concerning the worth of the university in today's world, this volume will have served its purpose.

NATHAN M. PUSEY

Cambridge, Massachusetts.
May 27, 1963

* * * * * * *

CONTENTS

* * * * * * *

THE AGE OF
THE SCHOLAR

* * * * * * *

* * * * * * *

A FAITH FOR THESE TIMES

In asking me to share in the opening convocation of the Harvard Divinity School, Professor George H. Williams, the acting Dean, mentioned that the last participation of a president of the University in an exercise of the Divinity School had been in 1909. I was immediately curious to see what this presidential valedictory had been like. I found that it was the address President Eliot gave at the close of the eleventh session of the Harvard Summer School of Theology in July 1909—an address entitled "The Religion of the Future."

President Eliot's text suggests at least one reply to those people who have been insisting on Harvard's neglect of religion. For if one were to define religion as he apparently did it is abundantly clear that this University was not, never has been, and is not now, irreligious at all. On the contrary.

There is evidence for President Eliot's own deep personal faith, and its nobility, in every line of his address, and it is possible—indeed it seems to me probable—that this faith not only animated many of the people at work in the University in his time but that it had done so for a long time both before and after, and that much of the University's present great stature is owed to it. For example, Mr. Eliot said in 1909, "The new religion will

Address at the opening convocation of the Harvard Divinity School, September 30, 1953, which also appeared as an article in *Harper's, Christian Century,* and other publications.

foster powerfully a virtue which is comparatively new in the world—the love of truth and the passion for seeking it." And again: "The workman today, who gets cut or bruised by a rough or dirty instrument, goes to a surgeon, who applies an antiseptic dressing to the wound, and prevents the poisoning. That surgeon is one of the ministers of the new religion. When dwellers in a slum suffer the familiar evils caused by overcrowding, impure food, and cheerless labor, the modern true believers contend against the sources of such misery by providing public baths, playgrounds, wider and cleaner streets, better dwellings, and more effective schools—that is, they attack the sources of physical and moral evil."

The word "moral" is slipped in rather unexpectedly at the end here and it may carry the argument a bit too far, but despite this there can be no doubt that President Eliot was a sincere and fervent believer in a religion that placed its greatest reliance on increased knowledge and good works. And I suspect further, as I have said, that a similar faith was widely held by members of this University in the period before the first World War when it was probably closer to an earlier Christian conviction than it was later to be, and that it has been held by many ever since. Judged by its fruits it has surely proved no inconsiderable faith, for it manifestly released, or at least expressed, a strong creative force that has been productive of much good both within the University and outside, and it seems to me beyond question, as I have said, that the present greatness of this University springs in no small measure from it. And yet I think it is no less true that by itself this faith will no longer do.

We might quarrel endlessly over the relationship between humanitarianism and high religion. There would be no profit in this. Let me then just state the following as a personal conviction and go on: that though our predecessors in President Eliot's generation were unquestionably men of great faith their faith will not do for us; if for no other reason, because events of the twentieth century have made its easy optimism unpalatable. For example, the passage about the passion for truth quoted above continued, "and the truth will progressively make men free; so that the coming generations will be freer, and therefore more productive and stronger than the preceding." We are not quite so sure about this as they were, and it is this uncertainty itself which constitutes our present greatest problem.

It is not that we do not have faith, or at least want to have faith, but that certainty escapes us, and that all things have been brought into doubt, and that fearing to be victimized we are inclined not to believe at all. We simply are not the "true believers" of whom President Eliot spoke, and this suggests that his was not a religion for the future. Something was left out of his account the absence of which has gone a long way toward vitiating his position. We must get hold of this something again in the midst of our present difficulties if we are to get on.

For President Eliot, the enemies to his true faith were churches, creeds, priests, anything supernatural, any concern for a life after death, anything that professed to be sacramental. I suspect, for example, though I do not know this, that he would have considered the doctrine central to generations of believers—that Christ came into the world to save sinners—as so much twaddle. His was to be a "simple and rational faith" and there was to be no place in it for "metaphysical complexities or magical rites."

We may overlook the disparaging conjunction of unequal things in the last phrase and observe simply that such things were not so easily to be gotten rid of: churches and creeds and metaphysical complexities persist, and we have need of them still. There has been ample time since 1909 to discover that you cannot get rid of things of this kind, or at least of the needs from which they spring, simply by turning your back on them or by pretending that they are not there. This is where President Eliot may have been wrong, at least wrong for our time, for it has now become frighteningly clear that if you try to ignore metaphysical considerations (I would say consideration of ultimate things) or cover them up in bursts of energy they will rise up in perverted and distorted forms to mock your thus too-circumscribed efforts. Nor was it right to have assumed, as President Eliot did, that if only one could get rid of churches and creeds, one would by that act also get rid of the human failings which had in the first place produced the blemishes irritating to him. Churchmen are not the only men who can be guilty of failures of imagination, understanding, and charity.

President Eliot had a creed, whether he admitted to it or not. It is there implicit in every line of his address. But in our time most of us will find this an inadequate one. What this proves, I think, is that our need was not then and is not now to get rid of creeds, but rather to examine into them, and now again, more especially, to find an adequate one for our time. We need to know, but we need also to believe; and what we want especially to do is to believe knowingly and to know with conviction.

President Eliot apparently would not, or could not, recognize that the old forms of Christianity which he was so ready to depreciate, and which, as they had been latterly abused, rightfully irritated him, had at one time been vehicles for holding and transmitting truth—that is, for communicating profound and relevant insights about the human situation—from one generation to another. And what he did not suspect was that in getting rid of the forms we ordinary citizens would also run the risk of getting rid of the insights, and that we would, in fact, then in surrendering to a new kind of blindness or idolatry, run the risk of cutting ourselves off from a whole, possibly even the most central, area of human experience. He was wrong, I think, in urging his generation to get rid of what he called "paganized Christianity" by eschewing metaphysics and by escaping into a formless empyrean of good will. It would have been better to have exhorted them, rather, while keeping a firm grasp on the spiritual treasure that had been transmitted to them, to wrestle more vigorously toward a fresh understanding of "first things." At any rate it seems to me we must do this. Our need is not for a religion for the future but for religion now, since the vigorous and creative faith which Eliot and his generation had has in considerable measure spent its force, and in many areas, in many minds, a paralyzing disbelief has taken its place. A new effort of the human mind and heart and will is thus called for, and this, it seems to me, is where students of theology in this school and in schools of this kind come in. For, "if the trumpet give an uncertain sound, who shall prepare himself to the battle?"

Out of our present great need a renewal must come. I do not mean to imply that we can lift ourselves by our own boot straps, but I am ready to insist that we can now study in areas too long neglected, can at least a little relax our wills and our zealotry, and can learn again to listen and to let ourselves be helped.

It has been my experience that when one inquires today about religious questions—at least outside professional circles—one is apt normally to be met with disinterest, ignorance, and apathy on the one hand and too often, where interest does exist, with ignorance and fanaticism on the other. We have not been well taught about religion, and there is as a consequence a very widespread religious illiteracy and correspondingly little religious practice. Perhaps as pupils we have been inclined to be unteachable. But I do not want to slip into President Eliot's error here by seeming to imply that all that is lacking is knowledge. It is rather, I think, faith.

Personal religion and understanding of and participation in the work of the Church could apparently in many earlier generations be taken for granted. Latterly they have tended to ebb away in the all but universal adoration of the State, and in almost idolatrous preoccupation with the secular order, with the accumulation of knowledge, and with good works. There is not, and cannot be, a quarrel with any of these things in themselves, but only with the notion that they are independently sufficient goods. And it is because they have been tried and the people are still not fed that the theological student of today is presented with an immense, new, and most difficult responsibility.

There is an almost desperate urgency for schools of religion vigorously to do something fresh and convincing to meet the present need. It is leadership in religious knowledge, and even more, in religious experience—not increased industrial might, not more research facilities, certainly not these things by themselves—of which we now have a most gaping need. And it is because of this that you who have chosen to study religion and to give your lives to the ministry stand again where many times before your illustrious predecessors have stood, in the very center of the fight. Andover Hall is not on the periphery of Harvard University, it is not remote from any region where the serious business of men is done, and it cannot be permitted to become so.

Harvard was begun at least in part, as you know, because

our earliest predecessors were afraid lest they leave an illiterate ministry behind them. Certainly no one is going, or ever intended, to argue for an illiterate ministry; but if we think as Eliot did of all who do the world's work as ministers, regardless of what they know or care for God, perhaps that is what we have been getting. Our more immediate predecessors were inclined to think you can serve God through many careers other than that of the formal ministry. In this they were completely right. But it does not necessarily follow that in these other careers, any more than in the formal ministry itself, one necessarily serves God. We need to know what we are doing and how best to do it.

It is my very sincere hope therefore that theological studies can here be given a fresh impetus and a new life within this University. It is to be hoped, too, that such an augmented effort in this direction will result in more able and dedicated young men coming into the ministry, and that a changing climate of opinion will then make it possible for those who have chosen this path to lead fully significant and effective lives in a new and more Christian society.

Theology should not be thought of as a minor intellectual exercise among other intellectual exercises; certainly not only this. It is expected to carry an answer to our deepest hungers and need. The student of theology comes to a university to grow in the knowledge but also the love of God, and should leave the university with a will steadfastly to help others to do the same.

I do not wish to argue that there is any Christian truth different from truth itself. But it is necessary to recognize that truth can be lost in a formless and uninformed faith, and that we can no longer get along in the face of our present great needs with such. The university must always serve truth, but we must make a fresh effort and learn again to do this more fully. Eliot's insight did not encompass the whole of it; another man's will not either, but we must go on trying, freshly and creatively, in humility and in love, and with all the allies we can find. It is to be hoped, therefore, that we can now here have a revitalized school of religious learning, and that its influence will be increasingly felt throughout the whole University.

A member of the Harvard Divinity faculty said here a few years ago that "faith is the consciousness that moral values and spiritual experiences have a sacred character." It is more of this consciousness that we most desperately need, and that, difficult as it may seem to be epistemologically, we must learn again to know by faith with thanksgiving. There are many who will join with me in the hope expressed here today that in this effort Harvard—especially the faculty and the graduates of this school—will again lead the way.

* * * * * * *

EDUCATION IN THE PUBLIC EYE

IN MY OPINION much of the outside criticism currently directed against our educational enterprise is misguided, uninformed, unproductive, unwarranted, and unnecessary. At Harvard, for example, amidst all the recent recrimination and fomented suspicion there is no one who can or will come forward to name a single Communist among our three thousand teachers. And yet some unfriendly critics continue to belabor us with the name of one single teacher who once was a Communist, seeking thereby to create the impression—or perhaps mistakenly believing—that we are a seat for widespread disloyalty. It will be well for everyone, for American education, and for our country, when this sort of thing shall have run its course.

But what are the criticisms that arise from within? These are much more serious, but also, fortunately, of a more promising and productive kind. We who are involved in education worry a great deal, almost incessantly it seems to me, about what we are doing. It is my impression that we are always asking ourselves with troubled brow, What is the effect of the whole educational enterprise? It is not that we are afraid we are producing people who are disloyal to our country. We know that despite a few widely exploited examples to the contrary, this is not

Shortened version of an address, "Criticism and Reaffirmation," before the New England Association of Colleges and Secondary Schools, Boston, December 4, 1953.

true. But we are deeply and perennially concerned lest we
are producing people unworthy of the great opportunity
for high achievement given them with the gift of life, and
so incapable either of deeply valuing or understanding
and then of furthering, continuing, and advancing the
insights and articles of faith that have brought us where we
are. We know that parents are apt to be too much concerned with the jobs their children are to get, and that
educational considerations are therefore too easily turned
away from the big considerations to what are thought to
be immediately practical ends. But we who are involved in
the work of education, on the other hand, want our schools
and colleges to produce not just doctors, or merchants, or
lawyers, or engineers, or whatever it may be—and certainly
not just faultfinders—but above all, and essentially, free
men capable of thinking for themselves: believing men,
knowledgeable men, steadfast and concerned and decent
men in ever increasing numbers, who will recognize and
maintain and develop quality at every point in our national life—at every point in every community—whether
this be thought of as a standard to which we repair (as
some would have it) or as an added flavor that will come
to grace our sincerest efforts. We in education have to
produce these people—we have to *be* these people—out of
rather recalcitrant material, and it is in the face of this
responsibility, not at the vastly exaggerated issue of
loyalty or disloyalty, that our chief misgivings arise.

We are not sure we are producing as fine or as steadfast
people as we might. We wish we might do our job better.
What we wonder about is how we are going to do this. A
typical most urgent consideration before us at the moment
therefore, as we brood about this task, is clearly how we
can get more and abler people to help us. The need for
more primary teachers has been aired in the press for some

time. Now the yawning need has moved on to the secondary school level, and soon it will be felt in the colleges.
We need more teachers than we have, and one way or
another we must work to get them. But it is just as clear
that it is the quality and character these teachers are to
show that is of chief importance, and we are rightfully
uneasy about this. Fortunately, now, college after college
which twenty-five years and more ago turned away dis-
dainfully from the responsibility of producing people who
would gladly teach anywhere outside of that same, or some
other, college or university, is now turning back, recognizing anew its obligation toward the whole of education,
affirming again and setting out to do something about
meeting the need for more liberal, for more substantial—
as opposed to technical and mechanical—education at
every level. These colleges have always, according to their
lights, been trying to produce liberally educated, humane,
and concerned people. What they have to do more aggres-
sively now is to try to produce such people who will look
at teaching as an honorable and exciting and demanding
career, and who will see in education a new frontier for
American life. Happily, a widening number are making
the effort to do so.

A more vexatious worry among us than the supply of
teachers has to do with the kind of education we are to
provide. The basic difficulty here seems always to turn on
whether we are to think in terms of an educational program designed to be manageable by everyone in an age
group or whether we are to try to maintain one that will
test and stir the ablest and most enterprising of our young
people. Arguments can be and are advanced on both sides
of this question interminably. Unfortunately it is not a
particularly fruitful discussion, for in fact we have always
to do both things, and both things are worth doing. Our

educational system must provide educational opportunity and experience, as the reports so frequently say, for all American youth; but we cannot stop there or rest too quickly, for it cannot be permitted to do this in terms only of a mass and so at the expense of its other function, which is a perpetual requirement to discover and develop talent, and this not only for the happiness of the individuals involved but also, of course, for the common good.

The best sort of teacher is always concerned to find the peculiar quality and ability in each of his students. It is an endless and difficult and fascinating job. And then he seeks to develop this where he can and to encourage its possessor to go on until he shall have learned to make the fullest use of his gift and so have come into the completest possible personal awareness of life. For it is the variety and richness of personality itself which is the great wonder and the great glory of our world. At an early stage of education it is perhaps possible to reconcile this kind of activity with the responsiblity to provide for all youth, but as time goes on, it becomes increasingly difficult to keep both objectives in mind. Concession one way or the other has to be made.

Some of us feel that in recent years too much concession has been made in adapting educational programs to the needs of the largest numbers of students; others feel that our procedures are still too narrowly designed for the few. So expressed, merely in terms of numbers, the argument is misstated. What we are really concerned for is quality in mental activity, the furtherance of the capacity and the desire to take in knowledge and to use it, the actual achievement of knowledge, and the engendering of the desire to go on learning and to live in the light of learning. It is at this point that our misgivings arise—we may even incline to despair—for we are not at all sure we are succeeding as fully as we might. There is too much in our public life, after centuries of educational effort, to give us pause. But certainly the answer here is not more concession.

As the educational system rises from the earliest grades up through the universities there must be a heightened concern for quality, and more and more attention must be given to the needs of the more talented and willing students. At the college level improved scholarship and recruitment programs are being developed toward this end to eliminate some of the difficulties that have long stood in our way. All through the educational program it is to be hoped that counseling services will become less and less concerned with immediate vocational considerations; less concerned, that is, to decide prematurely for a young person what he should do to earn his living than to help him to see what he can make of himself, what he might become, and especially what role knowledge and learning can have in this process.

It can be seen already from what has been said that without help from the outside we are ourselves rather insistent and vigorous critics of the educational enterprise and have misgivings about what we are doing. There is another point at which we are ready to find fault. We have a haunting doubt, especially perhaps at those levels where our attention to knowledge and learning has gone furthest and been most faithful, that we have not done as much as we should have done in finding ways to forge some vital link in students between what they know and what they do. To some, current educational practices seem to be too largely directed toward a student's active self; to others, toward his knowing, rational self. I am sure extreme and condemnatory examples of both practices can be found. But so long as the student keeps his knowledge in one compartment and goes on living in response to wants and desires that have not been shaped, perfected, or directed by his knowledge—ignorantly and irresponsibly—so long some sense of futility and concern must continue to attach to what we are doing. And too often this seems to be the case.

Here is a widespread kind of disloyalty—disloyalty at the level of behavior—to the finest insights, ideas, and practices in our tradition; disloyalty to reasonableness, freedom, kindliness, initiative, precision, taste, and magnanimity—about which we have abundant reason to be concerned and about which, of course, we are concerned. We have not done so well here as we might, either in an early age, when our efforts are said to have been addressed almost exclusively to the knowing self, or now, when we endeavor to take much fuller recognition of the forces other than knowledge that operate in students' lives but have not yet become really skillful in bringing them into mutual play and interaction with their knowing minds. Here again we are not presented with a choice between alternatives but are confronted with an urgent necessity in our educational practices to find ways to modulate and fuse things that have been too often held apart.

I should like parenthetically to suggest here that to my way of thinking the best avenue for making progress at this point lies through the humanities. For what is needed is a greater play of the imagination in learning than we have been getting. Bearing down with the knowing mind on a specific fact is important, indeed indispensable, but not in itself sufficient. From that point an awareness must arise and widen out that draws the inclination of the whole person with it—an awareness of the affections and the heart as well as the head—through the attractiveness and warmth with which the imagination alone can irradiate it. This is perhaps where we have done too little. It is not just in pursuit of the humanities that the imagination can be cultivated, but certainly there it is of the essence; for if ever art speaks to young people, or to any people, it must speak through the instrumentality of the imagination to whole persons.

And there is one step further here where our self-criticisms take us. We are not completely without misgiving concerning the capacity our students acquire for commitment. We have here, too, a haunting feeling that we may have left this matter too much to chance. It is not something with which we can deal easily and directly; but it is just as clearly not a consideration to be met with indifference. This matter merges into the other. Since it is not just where our students' heads are that must worry us, but where their hearts are also, perhaps here too art can be our best ally, and through it we can move finally into religion.

I have tried to suggest that all is not well with the world of education any more than all is well with the climate of opinion that surrounds us—indeed have tried to suggest that the latter owes something to the former. We are subject to much criticism from the outside, and we engender no inconsiderable amount of it within by ourselves.

A few things may perhaps be said in summary:

American education has set for itself the goal of developing free men. That is to say, its major purpose is to train people who are able to think for themselves, exercise judgment and act upon that judgment, and deeply care. This is not easy, and we do it imperfectly, but surely the way to do this is not by indoctrinating or seeking to inculcate some particular point of view. Individuality and variety and free investigation—not conformity—are of the very essence of democratic life and of democratic education.

Today there appear to be a rather large number of people who are frightened because of the freedom American education enjoys. And there are people, including ourselves, who are dissatisfied with the progress we have made. Some in the face of the threat of totalitarianism now appear inclined to feel that our schools and colleges should become centers for indoctrination. This surely would be to lose the greatest battle of this century without a fight. Americanism does not mean enforced and circumscribed belief; it cannot mean this. We know that free men are developed not by indoctrination but only by that superlative kind of gifted teaching which can engender fresh thought and living concern.

It would be a sorry thing if in resisting totalitarianism we were to follow the counsels of the frightened and adopt its methods. It is rather for us now to look again at the high purpose we serve, not to absolve our former failures and shortcomings, but to renew our faith in what we are doing, to get a firmer grasp of the goal, and to go ahead.

Our job is to educate free, independent, and vigorous minds capable of analyzing events, of exercising judgment, of distinguishing facts from propaganda and truth from half-truths and lies, and—in the most creative of them at least—of apprehending further reaches of truth. It is also our responsibility to see that these minds are embedded in total persons who will stand with faith and courage, and always, too, in thoughtful concern for others. We must all of us, at every level in education, work together to do this job. The vast majority of people in this country want us to do this, and not some other task. I would suggest only to any of our critics who may have been confused or wavering on the matter of how the goal is to be won that, at least at the level of education with which I am most immediately concerned, the way to achieve the desired end is not by harrassing professors, or by seeking to turn universities into little police states rather than free associations of scholars, or by governing boards' surrendering their responsibilities to the pressures of hysteria or reckless attacks. The way is quite other than this. And I believe the matter is essentially no different at the level of the schools.

American education has a very fine, if not entirely unblemished, record of achievement behind it. In times of tension and confusion such as the present the obligation upon us all is greater than ever before to hold fast to its central purpose and historic role of serving the truth, working first and always to produce free men, and maintaining a spirit of hope. There is now an especially urgent obligation upon our universities to preserve freedom of inquiry and freedom of teaching, but it is no less upon our schools and colleges. Together we must continue to demonstrate and defend our heritage of freedom, support creative thinking for the advance of civilization, and serve as the foundation, the creators and defenders, of liberty in a free people, and now, as always, be the leaders in the fight against totalitarianism.

We are indeed today in the public eye. Let us acquit ourselves like free men.

* * * * * * *

FREEDOM, LOYALTY, AND THE
AMERICAN UNIVERSITY

A MODERN UNIVERSITY has two principal activities
—teaching and research. The first part of its obligation is to
keep knowledge alive, usable, and growing: the other essential part is to help to prepare young people for responsible
living and for all of the great callings of life. Any other
activities the university may have (and they are many)
rightfully develop from one or another of these primary
responsibilities—to advance learning and to perpetuate it
to posterity.

But a university's influence reaches far beyond the students and teachers within its walls and the community of
which they are a part. It works outward through various
agencies, chiefly through the great family of those who
were once a part of the institution and are now graduated,
people who are involved in virtually every part of the
whole human enterprise. And since there are many universities and hundreds and hundreds of colleges across the
country these institutions of higher education come in one
way or another to affect almost everyone's life, and should
be of interest to many others than those immediately concerned.

For the past year and a half universities have been accorded unusual attention in the nation's press—more at-

Address before the National Press Club, Washington, D.C., May 25,
1954.

tention, or at least often a different kind of attention, than they would like. Since the picture one might have formed from this discussion seems to me likely to be a very distorted one, and since during the past eight months I have been in an especially favored position to become familiar with the inner workings of one of our great American universities, I should like today from that experience to suggest what a true portrait of a university might be. I must talk primarily about Harvard, but I should like to think what I have to say about this university applies, at least in considerable part, to others as well.

Harvard University is a populous place. In round numbers there are ten thousand students, three thousand teachers, and another four thousand or more people who serve the University in a multitude of capacities. Many of these people are married and have families. The Harvard community may therefore be said to comprise in any given year more than twenty thousand individuals. It is the equivalent of a good-sized American community. It is also necessary to remember that there is considerable change in this group every year. Thousands graduate each spring and move away, others accept positions elsewhere and move on. At the same time an equal number of new people come into the community as students, teachers, or in some other capacity. It is probable that at least forty to fifty thousand individuals lived and worked at Harvard during the past twenty years, and at least as many again were trained there for military duties during the war. No one enters without some one, or usually several qualified people, first passing judgment on his qualifications for membership. Out of the large number of new people who come each fall, only very few stay on permanently in the Harvard community. Most remain for one, two, or perhaps as much as five or six years. In an average year probably no more than thirty or forty achieve permanent appointments. All American communities are mobile; none more so than our universities.

How does a person gain membership on the Harvard faculty or that of any other American university? A brief discussion of the organization and nature of a university may serve to suggest why the Harvard Corporation was reluctant to dismiss a certain associate professor whose name was much in the press some months ago. It may also throw at least a little light on the touchy question of academic freedom, though I hesitate to introduce this phrase which now has a strange power to arouse violent feeling, is widely misunderstood, and is often given implications which were never originally intended.

The idea that a scholar must be free to follow his own hunches in pursuing his special studies is not the whim of some modern educator. It comes down to us through the whole history of learning, back at least as far as the medieval universities. It is not primarily a question of "freedom." Certainly it is not, nor was it ever intended to be, a question of academic "privilege." A scholar or scientist has an *obligation* to investigate and report new ideas in his field, even when his conclusions may be unpopular among the general public or among his own colleagues. Time after time, in the progress of our Western world, it has been the work of a single scholar, doggedly holding out against the set prejudices of others, that has given us the great new idea which has advanced our knowledge of ourselves and of our world. Because this has happened, we hope it will go on happening. It is our determination within the universities to keep the possibility alive. On the other hand, because of thoughts that are now in our minds, let me say at once that freedom of scholarly inquiry would, of course, be completely vitiated by adherence to international communism, where every individual, even the scholar, must subordinate himself to party doctrine.

The making of an American scholar or a scientist is a long slow process. He must study for three or four or five years after finishing college before he is accepted at all in his own field. Then comes a trial period of five to ten years in the laboratory or study, and in the classroom. During all this time, in all our great universities, a man holds minor ranks—teaching fellow, instructor, assistant professor. When he has been through this long grind of training and testing, the day comes when the question of a permanent appointment for him is to be raised and he is to be judged finally as a scholar or a scientist. At Harvard, at this point, committees of his seniors, both in his own institution and elsewhere, study his record and weigh it against that of others. If he passes this test, he becomes an associate professor or a professor, a real member of the "community of scholars," the kind of association that has come down to us from the Middle Ages and forms the heart of a university. At this point he gets an appointment for life, subject in the case of Harvard to removal only for "grave misconduct or neglect of duty." These men holding life appointments are then expected to become the field generals, so to speak, in man's quest for knowledge, the men who lead our system of free inquiry and who train the men who in the future will carry on this great tradition of seeking to add to knowledge.

Now despite this careful screening process a few men pass this final test who turn out to be disappointments, one way or another. Some suffer debilitating illness or personal loss or disappointment that saps the zest the job requires. Some just cease to produce or go off on tangents. Occasionally a scholar proves to be a "one big idea" man who never again duplicates his early brilliant promise. Such people are a small minority, but they, too, have their place and belong, and by their presence serve to call attention to the freedom and responsibility that make a university great.

The way of a scholar is often a challenging, lonely journey. He usually works alone without much attention or encouragement from others. But it is of the greatest importance that he know—have unequivocal assurance—that whatever he finds and reports, within the limits of his own knowledge and skill, will not penalize him as a man. If he sees men around him dismissed from their positions for less than the most serious reasons—because of popular clamor, or on anything less than the most solid proof—it would not be surprising if he were then to shirk his own basic responsibility in the field of learning. It is for this reason that every individual case affecting one professor—and I would underscore this—every individual case affecting one professor is, in a sense, a test of the very idea of the university as we have known it through the centuries. The governing boards of any institution have a responsibility to preserve the nature of the university by seeing to it that no man is dismissed except for the most serious reason, and then only on substantial proof of the facts alleged.

And in view of this statement let me offer it as my opinion, in passing (and I may do this because the basic decisions were taken before I was called to be Harvard's president), that it is a credit to the governing boards of Harvard that they dealt with charges of communism exactly as they would deal with any other serious charge against a man. They said they would not have a man under communist discipline in their employ. But they also showed that they would not lightly dismiss a man on unproved charges and against his own unchallenged testimony that he is not a Communist.

It is to be hoped always that we will learn from the experiences of others. The great tradition of the German universities which so significantly influenced the development of American higher education came to full flower when the supervisory force of government was benevolent and generous. But often at the peak of the German reputation, when the Kaiser still wore the German crown, there was government opposition to appointing professors in the universities who were not politically orthodox or socially acceptable. Some historians have argued that the scientific achievements of Germany in the century before Hitler were made in spite of official intervention in university affairs. Certainly the seeds of educational authoritarianism were planted long before Hitler. In the days of the Federal Republic, three years before Hitler came to power, the German historian Ludwig Bernhard commented, "Whether the new state will recognize the powerful aid which *free* universities can give to the thriving of a people, or will go the easier way of suppression and regimentation, cannot be foreseen with certainty." Three years later, to the world's distress, the way was sadly obvious.

Harvard has now come, in company with several other similar American institutions, to a position in the forefront of the world's great universities. If Harvard is great today it is not just because of its distinguished faculty, its unusual libraries, its well-equipped classrooms and laboratories. Its present position also owes much to the farsightedness of the people who built the institution we now enjoy. Harvard is great primarily because of what it has stood for through the years—a bulwark in the maintenance of freedom of the mind, that freedom upon which all the other freedoms depend. It is great because it has repeatedly stood for this at times when it would have been quite easy to forget its responsibility to defend and maintain the university idea.

This main point of what a university is and stands for may not always get through to every one of the thousands and thousands of individuals who come into a university for varying periods of time. Undoubtedly not everyone honors it and continues loyal to it as he should. But clearly the overwhelming majority of those who are touched by a university's influence come to understand and have a passionate allegiance to the free way of life. This does not mean license. It does not mean lack of concern for country or for the ordinary activities of all people. It means only the responsibility to use one's mind as best one can in the service of truth; and it is, of course, the people who have learned this who are the lifeblood of democracy. Such people are nobody's men. They do not bow to hysteria like reeds in a shifting wind, nor do they give in to autocratic pressure. They are the very antithesis of the kind of persons who would succumb to communism or any other kind of totalitarianism.

Universities, founded on this basic idea, are among our nation's greatest assets. Harvard's own contribution to American society during more than three hundred years in terms of the free men who have in her halls acquired the knowledge and will to serve their country is beyond the telling. I have tried on several occasions to give some indication of it. Teachers, lawyers, writers, industrial leaders, scientists, men in government—tens and tens of thousands of devoted, loyal, able people woven into the very fabric of the life of this nation. It is they in their multitude, not the occasional aberrant, one should look at. They are men of differing tastes and opinions, but, as President Eliot once said, "intensely democratic in temperament," the kind who in peace stand "firmest for the public honor and renown" and in war plunge "first into the murderous thickets."

In the Memorial Church at Harvard are the names of nearly four hundred of her sons who died in World War I; nearly seven hundred in World War II. Harvard lost nearly thirty in Korea. Whenever the United States has needed Harvard's intellectual and physical strength the University has not been found wanting. More than 45,000 military men were trained at Harvard during World War II. Harvard's laboratories turned from what is commonly called "pure research" to the actual application of abstract discoveries in war problems. The oxygen mask carried by Jimmie Doolittle over Tokyo was developed at Harvard's School of Public Health. Thousands of military men had reason to give thanks for a little pamphlet on survival in the tropics prepared by a young Harvard botanist. At Harvard's Radio Research Laboratory, six hundred scientists from all over the United States were brought together to work on radar countermeasures and radio jamming problems. In another famous laboratory, experts in psychological, linguistic, and accoustical factors devised methods for increasing human efficiency under conditions of stress. At the Underwater Sound Laboratory were born many of the devices which helped the Allies win the battle beneath the surface of the seas. Harvard scientists were in the forefront of new discoveries in ballistics with the building and improvement of large-scale calculating machinery; in the development of the atomic bomb; and in the application of chemistry to incendiary devices. Harvard's President was a leader in the mobilization of scientific manpower that had so much to do with the success of our war effort.

At the same time that much of Harvard's energy was devoted to the problem of defeating the enemy, there was going on work of long-term benefit to human life, like important techniques used in the donation, fractionation, and preservation of blood. Such are only a few of the products that flow from the minds and efforts of university teachers in time of special need. There are many others.

Since the advent of the cold war, Harvard has been operating a Russian Research Center which has already added greatly to our understanding of the Russian and his potential. Talent in all fields of human knowledge has been brought to bear on such subjects as Russian education, science, law, government, communications, terror tactics. Out of this work there have come scores of special studies and a dozen major volumes of wide significance, and the work is just beginning.

But the physician today advocates preventive medicine as well as diagnosis. In addition to our knowledge of Russian communism we should seek to prevent its outbreak in this country by attacking it at the roots. One way is to turn out well-balanced, intelligent citizens, which Harvard aims to do. Another is to stamp out the germs of communism bred in ignorance, ill health, economic stress, and social unrest.

In countless undramatic ways these things are being done at Harvard. Its laboratories and associated hospitals have been pursuing such fundamental problems as the causes and cures for malnutrition, cancer, poliomyelitis, heart ailments, and so on. Historians and government and language specialists join with public health experts and educators to study the irritations of colonial peoples and the needs of underdeveloped countries. Economists and students of business search for ways to maintain a dynamic economy while encouraging stability.

Independent investigations in various parts of the University often bear on the same topic. Juvenile delinquency, commonly adjudged to be a dangerous source of social and political instability, receives attention at Harvard at several points. At the Graduate School of Education a principal effort is directed at improving school systems and teaching methods. At the Law School are the psycho-legal approaches of the Gluecks and the studies of the judiciary. In the medical areas of the University, research is directed to winning the battle against diseases of childhood. At the same time, experts from the Medical School, the School of Public Health, the Children's Medical Center, the Harvard Department of Social Relations, the Judge Baker Guidance Center, and other community social agencies cooperate in the field of child psychiatry—in research into the cause, treatment, and prevention of juvenile delinquency and in the training of personnel to deal with delinquents. Harvard assists in the operation of numerous well-baby and well-child clinics, where crises in family life may be detected before they become court cases. There are few greater problems facing us at the moment than the need for increased family stability. And finally, at Harvard University, hundreds of undergraduates, and many graduate students too, participate in the social-service program of Phillips Brooks House and give their time to young people through boys' clubs, Sunday schools, Y's, Scout troops, and local hospitals.

A university in its ideal condition is a free association of free men. This is what it was in its origin in Europe in the Middle Ages. This is what it tries to be now. It is a place where older men seek, study, inquire; where they are free to do this because the results of such inquiries have been shown again and again to be those things which make life good for all men. It is a place where young people come to live and work and learn from their elders, and then, when their capacities enable them to do so, continue the labor of learning and investigation leading to a fuller life for us all. From the dreams and thoughts and efforts of scholars during centuries have come a ceaseless flood of new ideas, of experiences made meaningful, of increased understanding, new hopes and promises that have combined to make what we call civilization. It has taken many people—many kinds of people—in many countries and communities to bring us as far as we have come. But basic to it all has been free inquiry, the idea that is the center and the life force of a university.

One cannot create or maintain such a place as a university in an atmosphere of fear and restriction. The free spirit that produces the new insight and the step forward quickly dies under such circumstances. This is why a university could not succumb to communism and remain a university. This is why universities will always be in the forefront of the fight against evil of this kind. No one knows this better than those who live in, have learned from, and have chosen to give their lives to universities. This is why there is such determination on the part of the boards of control at Harvard that in dealing with a single or even a few aberrants care must be taken not to surrender or injure the whole way of life from which alone must come the good this university can do. This is why Harvard's care in dealing with the four cases within its community may have seemed oversolicitous to those less familiar with and less responsible for the life-giving pattern of freedom on which the whole strength, the whole productivity, of a university depends.

We need feel no uncertainty about Harvard's, nor any other university's, attitude toward communism. Harvard wants no part of it. Nor do the others. Inasmuch as communism seeks to control and dictate to men's minds, communism is any true university's inevitable enemy. The

Harvard Corporation has stated that Harvard wants no one who has given up his conscience to Communist discipline. Such a man lacks the necessary independence of thought and action. Nothing could be more opposed to everything that communism stands for than a free university, and we believe that Harvard's record—and the record of the whole of American education—is one in which the nation can take tremendous pride.

There are numerous large considerations facing us, the citizens of the United States. But in my opinion for the long run there is no more serious necessity upon us than to find an adequate number of really qualified teachers for all levels of the educational enterprise in the United States in the decades immediately ahead—knowledgeable leaders who will think, work, and be able to win response in young people. Enrollments in the elementary schools began to break out of existing facilities almost ten years ago. They continue to swell. Now the problem has moved on to the high schools. Soon it will be in the colleges. Where there were two of us in the schools a little while ago, now there are more than three. People have been alerted to the need for buildings, but this is not the most serious part of the problem. There was no surplus of excellent teachers in our time. Where is a new enlarged supply to come from? Especially where will these teachers come from if thoughtless and extravagant attacks, made in almost complete disregard of honest effort to see things as they are, continue and thus discourage able young people from going into teaching?

To single out teachers from among other groups of the population, to subject them to an exceptional kind of accounting, seems to me to be little better than scapegoating. If there is anything I should like to say to the American people about the current situation in education it would be to urge them not to be misled by those who would exploit a few very exceptional and quite atypical examples for personal advantage. Educators at every level have shown themselves well aware of the Communist problem and have demonstrated their ability to cope with it.

American education works to produce free, independent, thoughtful, and concerned citizens. It has always done this, and still does. If it sometimes falls short of its highest aim, so do other efforts. But the need for such people grows greater every day. People in every community in the United States should be working not to abuse but to strengthen the educational enterprise. To tear down is not the way to set about this very urgent job. This is not a time to seek to exploit for private gain feelings of insecurity, nor a time to work out personal fears and frustrations at the expense of other classes or professional groups. It is a time, rather, when all who truly love this country should unite to work with teachers, in friendship, trust, and cooperation, through education to help the United States to continue to grow toward its great promise.

* * * * * * *

EDUCATION FOR FREE MEN

EDUCATION came into our national life almost at the same time as church and state. In a very real sense it was always there, for to be a human being is constantly to be suffering and inflicting education. The most basic education has probably always gone on and still today goes on, well or badly, in the family. But our early ancestors in this country were not content to leave this important matter without making explicit provision for formal education. As early as 1635 the town of Boston voted that "our brother Mr. Philemon Pormort shalbe intreated to become scholemaster for the teaching and nourtering of children with us." By 1636 a college was founded at public expense, and soon free grammar schools became an established fact in the Massachusetts Bay Colony.

From these small beginnings the extension of organized education has gone on. Sometimes it has progressed under the press of necessity, sometimes in free response to a new and challenging insight. With help, even with opposition, it has still advanced until it has reached its present multiform, bewildering shape. Today it would take a cartographer of incredible wizardry to delineate even the physical facilities now devoted across the nation to education. Were such a one to try also to represent in graphic form the varied aims, practices, degrees of effectiveness, con-

Address before the Public Education Association, New York, October 20, 1954.

flicting purposes, the different levels, methods, modes of control, theories, curricula and all the rest, the result would be a picture of incomprehensible complexity.

For this reason it was a wise precaution—or perhaps only a lucky accident—that led our predecessors to fix and keep local the responsibilities for schools. Though this placed a heavy and inescapable task on local groups, in general it has provided in its very variety a source of strength and richness, despite lamentable inequalities between one community and the next. We do not have a national system of education; we do not have one way of educating. Though this may seem to other peoples a casual method of providing for such an important matter, in general it has led with us to life, and away from the deadening track of uniformity. It is well that education is not primarily the business of the state, nor of a special group within the state, nor primarily a concern for professionals, though it must always rely in some measure on all three. It is better that it is, in the United States, by intention, something that all citizens are expected to benefit from and to be concerned and responsible for. I hasten to say at once, however, by way of qualification for the sake of all schoolmen, that citizens will rightfully discharge this responsibility for education not as meddlers, but rather as sympathetic, informed critics and helpers.

Though the public school's rapid proliferation—especially the spread of what we now call the comprehensive public high school—came only after 1870, today we are prepared to accept the public school as an essential part— seemingly an indigenous part—of almost every American community. Most of us owe an incalculable debt to one or several of these schools.

More than ninety per cent of young people are enrolled in the public schools. It is this basic and impressive fact which explains why, as President Conant pointed out several years ago, citizens must be interested in their schools, and why it is on the public schools, taken together, that we depend for two important functions. The first is to draw out the capacity and promise in our young people and keep social fluidity alive by helping each to his chance. The second is to nourish within our national life a sense of community. There is an especial strength for the United States, despite the problems created by numbers, in the fact that the public schools take in so many and do in effect therefore have a real chance to provide a common experience.

Education's role is commonly stated to be the conservation, extension, and perfection of the life of the community. There is room for much misunderstanding and difference of opinion at each of these points, but especially perhaps in the matter of perfection. What is meant by the expression "to perfect the life of the community"? Not infrequently this is interpreted as meaning simply to produce people in sufficient quantity with the necessary skills to keep our business and industrial life moving and growing. No one can honestly deny that education has this responsibility. And when we look at what is involved in discharging it at all the different levels, this is clearly seen in itself to be a staggering task, especially in these days when population increases have strained our facilities to the breaking point. But this surely is not all we have in mind when we come together to talk of education for free men. For free men at all occupational levels, if I may borrow some words from George Herbert, are not intended to "be drowned altogether in the works of their vocation, but sometimes [to] lift up their minds to better things, even in the midst of their pains."

Few if any other nations have ever tried to offer education to such a large percentage of its young people as we do. Our purpose has been no less than to provide schools for *all* American youth. Such a tremendous effort necessarily has involved difficulties so formidable for schoolmen that it is not surprising if all are not yet solved. Hence their need for our continuing sympathetic interest and help.

One of the most urgent early needs was for a widened curriculum to match the wider range of interest brought by increased kinds of young people coming into the schools. This change was understandably accompanied by deliberate turning away from an earlier emphasis on verbal education. Sometimes it was carried further to an actual disparagement of what was then referred to as "bookishness." Sympathetic as one must be with the difficulties confronting the schools, and proud as we all are of their achievement, when this point is reached it is perhaps possible to ask if all has been gain.

I am mindful at this moment of a woman teacher beside whom I once sat during a rather esoteric discussion of education. She taught in a large urban school system. The school in which she worked was in what we refer to euphemistically as a poorer district. It was desperately poor indeed. Furthermore, it was rent by the turmoil of a large migratory movement, fraught with dislocation, poverty, racial tension, and marred by almost every known kind of delinquency. The talk that evening was of great books, and I remember her leaning to me midway during the discussion and saying quietly, with what I am sure must have been incredible understatement, "This discussion does not have much to do with the situation where I live." I shall never forget that woman's remark.

There are indeed places within our systems of public schools that with reason seem almost hopeless, but if we are to think constructively about education, we cannot be put off by them—nor can we concentrate attention on numbers or physical facilities alone and, losing ourselves in such considerations, refuse to face up to the fact that education is in the end something that takes place in individuals and is concerned with minds. And so we come to the basic question confronting all who take thought for education: What should education—what may education, including public education—hope to be?

Formal education does not make minds. These are given from birth, and they grow whether we do anything about them or not. We cannot turn them off. Education's concern is rather with the use we make of them, what we can come in time to understand of their nature, and what we can do with them. It was a wholesome discovery of modern educational theorists that young people are customarily more active than thoughtful. But recognition of this fact should never obscure the more basic one that education addresses itself primarily to minds and has an inescapable mission to work always to bring action under the direction of thought. Though there is admittedly much pretension in our frequently reiterated claim that we in the schools produce free and self-reliant minds, this is nonetheless what we must always try to do.

A further qualification is needed at this point. It is easy in educational discourse to proceed on the assumption that the calculating, weighing, and assessing activity of our minds is separated from and independent of other factors and forces churning about within us, from other parts of our natures. It is possible to take too simple or too separate a view of what a mind is. We perhaps do better to talk of "selves" when we are trying to designate that something within us for which education is concerned, because the manner of thought of each of us, and our ways of acting, inevitably reflect the total person. It is not just with mind as an independent faculty that we have to be concerned, but with mind enmeshed in a deep, confused, and largely inarticulated emotional and spiritual life. Our aim is to make reason and generous feeling more effective within the fullness of self. This fact leads quickly to my main point.

Our mental personalities are formed and influenced by many things—by what we are given by nature, by the family situations in which we grow, by the whole impact of our culture. They are surely as various as are our external appearances. But some mental personalities are clearly more attractive than others, some have more grace within themselves and make more effective contributions in their manifold relationships. It is at least a part of the business of education to encourage this kind of excellence. Thus far perhaps we shall all agree. But the question then arises, how can education produce this result?

Though the variety in human nature will always demand a variety of approaches, there is evidence to suggest that some means are more effective than others, and in my judgment no more promising means has yet been found to produce intellectual excellence than the experience of good reading.

Basic to all but the most elementary learning is reading. This is undoubtedly why it is properly a matter of concern to teachers from the first grade throughout the whole of formal education. But what is not so widely recognized is that in most cases the quality or lack of quality in a mental life perhaps owes as much to what one customarily reads as to any other one thing. It is for this reason that though the simplest kind of reading may be acceptable fare for children at certain stages of their development, it is certainly not a sufficient staple for the intellectual fare of adults. Nor are newspapers or the average run of magazines sufficient by themselves—that is, apart from the supplementary influence of major books. Despite all our antipathy to "bookishness," there is a disturbing truth here which we shall overlook at our peril.

What we are depends in very considerable measure on the intellectual experiences we have had, or have not had —on the meaning we have found in life or have not found. Such experiences do not necessarily have to be found in books, but it is chiefly in books, in the best books, that the most illuminating human experiences are apt to be found —whether for the youngster discovering for the first time the joy of drifting down the river with Huck, or the adult, his radio or television silent for the moment, finding through books, in the bustle of contemporary America, some of the intellectual currents that have helped make him what he is.

If this be true, then to live apart from books is not to turn toward life but deliberately to cut one's self off from significant understanding of it. And this is what will happen if we turn too far from the verbal, that is from languages and literature in our educational practices. Books, as another has said, are men thinking. They are also at their best the work of the men whose thoughts are most worth knowing. For their thoughts are the kind of thoughts that can both engender in us joy in new awareness and stretch our thinking. In a very real sense we can only truly live and grow by such experiences.

Here is an emphasis in education which tends frequently to become obscured and which consequently needs repeatedly to be brought into clear view. For in the light it will be seen that the exclusive aim of education cannot be simply to impart information or to teach skills, or adjustment, or even citizenship, as we sometimes too readily assert; but that to all these must be added the more basic responsibility of trying to effect, even under the most dis-

couraging circumstances, a net increase in the role of the
intellect, and more especially in the quality of its influence
within the individual's life. There is involved here a necessity to give precision and control to thinking, but even
more, increased awareness, wider concern, some imaginative grasp of the heights and depths in human experience,
and in every situation with which the mind copes a reasonable concern for further relevancies. Nothing has yet been
shown more likely than the habitual reading of significant
literature to produce this result. Is it also possible, incidentally, that the widely lamented inability of recent
products of our schools adequately to express themselves
either orally or in writing is in some measure connected
with the relaxing of emphasis on this kind of reading in
the early grades?

The most difficult step in the whole process of educating
a human mind is to lift its possessor out of that unawak-
ened condition in which there has been not even a first
glimpse of the charm of learning or of the pleasures of the
mind. Because of man's proclivity for retrogression, it is
perhaps no less difficult to cause the experience to be repeated until it will carry life-long conviction. Yet this very
difficulty points unmistakably to what is the most serious
present need in education, public and private alike—the
need for a greater supply of teachers with imagination,
and learning, who themselves continue to find joy in these
things.

Schools, public schools no less than others, have always
had some great-souled teachers in their classrooms. All of
us—those of us who went to public school as well as those
who did not—can verify this from our own experience, for
all of us know at least a few individuals of more than usual
imagination, perceptiveness, patience, and determination

to whom our thanks are rightfully directed for the help they gave us as teachers. For the further increase of mental life in individuals, and through them in society, it is clear we need more people of this kind in our schools. The teacher's proper job is not to engender familiarity with the commonplaces of life, but to quicken awareness of its finer reaches and possibilities, to acquaint us with the excellent and the extraordinary that lie everywhere around us. But to do this the teacher must himself be sensitive to these things, which means chiefly, it seems to me, it is essential to have as teachers people who will go on caring about and reading books of quality all their lives.

Perhaps in the end what I am trying to say is only that poetry with its reach and with its concentration is as relevant in educational discussion as is psychology. Or as one Harvard professor said recently, "Wise men [should] take equal delight in the creative intelligence of scientist and of poet." Beyond this we must surrender the notion, if it is anywhere still held, that exacting intellectual experience cannot be attractive or enjoyable. Such experiences do not occur in the same way, or in the same amounts, or at all times for all people. But an education that does not give a young person at least some joy in intellectual experience will surely leave him completely unprotected against the abiding anti-intellectualism that lies within us all. This is most likely to happen in my judgment when education proceeds with inadequate attention to books. An education limited and made barren in this way is no proper education for men or states.

Two practical suggestions come to mind. If it is the aim of legislation governing the certification of teachers not so much to keep people out of the profession as to get superior individuals into it, it is perhaps time for an effort to be made in many states to remove restrictions which now prevent the full use of graduates of liberal-arts colleges in the classrooms of the public schools, elementary and secondary alike. It may very well be, however, that such changes will have also to be accomplished by new and more imaginative efforts to provide better in-service training. And second, perhaps the time has also come to try to effect changes to make it easier for experienced teachers to devote their efforts at summer school to their own intellectual interests rather than to further study of teaching methods. This is only to say that teachers should be encouraged, in my judgment, in all their experience to grow as persons rather than to become educational technicians.

In the United States the quality and well-being of education have been left largely to private citizens. We are quite mistaken if we lose patience because of this or assume it means making a compromise with mediocre achievement. It is still true that it is a good idea to make haste slowly. We have been a long time coming to where we are in education. We have done it through the constructive efforts of many people and have perhaps therefore built more soundly, certainly more generously, than has any other nation. We might get ahead faster for a while if all the problems of education were now to be solved by decree from the outside, if the means of realizing our hopes could be provided with liberality by governmental coercion, or if we were to take a more limited view of our responsibility. But this would scarcely be education for free men. It would certainly not be education of or by free men.

In the end, interested groups of private citizens in every locality and for every institution—I suspect no less for the "public" than the "private"—have still to do the job. There is nothing to do but go on, but it is possible now to do so with fresh resolve. For there is cause in our changed situation in the world to see new and exciting opportunities, and greater responsibilities, before American education than ever before.

America is her citizens. What they are—what they can become—depends upon her schools. It depends not least on the finest insights of our finest citizens, and on getting them understood and accepted. There should be no settlement here for a second best. There is a fullness of vision, a richness of life, that transcends ordinary awareness. It is time now through education to endeavor to make this operative in the lives of more and more of our people. Education for free men is what used to be called liberal education. If education is now to be made available to all, it is this kind of education, not some inferior version, that we should endeavor to provide.

To do so will obviously require a more considerable educational effort than has yet been made. One brand of skeptic will say it cannot be done; another will say it should not be done. But if the American citizen is now coming into the position of responsible leadership in the world where a procession of citizens of other lands have been before him, there will be tragedy and frustration and failure ahead if he is anything less than a liberally educated man.

Education working through individuals releases, cultivates, magnifies the power of reason and concern for others in human affairs. Though reason's victories are partial and its strength always tentative, it is—this side of God's assistance—the most attractive, most promising force we have. It is education's task to try to widen the area of reasonableness in private lives and public affairs, for without an appreciation of what reasonableness is, and the knowledge and will and patience to practice it, men do not deserve freedom.

Is it not with some such considerations as these in mind that we must set out to build a more promising kind of education for free men?

* * * * * * *

LEADERSHIP AND THE
AMERICAN UNIVERSITY

THE UNIVERSITY as we know it today in this country is of comparatively recent origin. Though the "name" was known and widely used, the "thing" waited upon the development of reputable graduate and advanced professional education. There were stirrings in this direction in several places during the seventies of the last century, some even earlier, but a convenient date now widely accepted for the start of full university education in America is the date of the founding of The Johns Hopkins University in 1876.

Both Brown and Harvard had been in existence a long time before this. I am certain, too, that their early work, even at the professional level, was neither inferior nor negligible. But different times call for new adaptations; and only as one reaches one objective does it become possible to reach beyond. Despite an extensive growth in the more distant past, the large sprawling, powerful modern American university which we know today came into being during the last seventy-five years, and has won its way to world esteem only within the last quarter century. The point demanding our attention here is that the period of

Subtitled "A Tribute to Henry M. Wriston," this address in somewhat greater length was delivered in Sayles Hall, Providence, Rhode Island, February 3, 1955, at a civic convocation marking the retirement of Mr. Wriston as President of Brown University.

the American university's growth largely coincided with the enormous—almost fabulous—industrial development of the United States, and that this juxtaposition, and consequent interpenetration, has had a great deal to do with determining the characters of both. This influence of one on the other now seems destined to increase rather than decline, and therefore raises a very serious question: Which is to exert the guiding pressure?

The influences—particularly the climate of ideas—that operated at the very beginnings of our oldest institutions of higher education appear at first glance to have been of a very different kind from those that seem pertinent today. Today it is against the background of the amazing economic structure of our national life, especially our urban industrial society, that we are inclined to see the university, possibly even there to seek its purpose and meaning. Then, however, it was weighed and discussed with reference first to the Church and second to the State—but, first and last, to Christ's Kingdom.

There is a new and very illuminating account of the intellectual background out of which a rationale for the oldest American university was first drawn together. I call attention to it because, since it occurs almost concealed in small print at the end of the recently published history of the Harvard Divinity School, I suspect it may very well have escaped wide attention. This is an excursus by George H. Williams, the present acting dean of the School, entitled "Church, Commonwealth and College—The Religious Sources of the Idea of a University."

It tells the story of how, in medieval Europe, as the university came into being and rose to self-consciousness, it sought to formulate a theoretical justification for itself as a kind of independent third force beside Church and State. The main purpose of Mr. Williams' article is to show how

this theoretical support was later taken over by the founders of Harvard College to justify the establishment and
define the role of the new institution for higher learning
they were building on these shores.

The arguments presented sound strange indeed to our
ears, for taken together or separately they do not provide
the kind of philosophical defense of a university one would
expect to hear today. Yet in so far as these early theorists
were concerned to secure the independence and autonomy
of the academic community, and also to ensure that in the
search for truth they would continue to cling fast to a
sense of moral and spiritual relevance, they were dealing
with matters which are, or at least should be, of considerable interest to us. For though the terms in which these
problems are stated have changed, the dangers remain.
First the university had to be established in independence
of the Church and of the State; a place had to be won for
the "prophet," or teacher, beside those of king and priest.
The university's defenders therefore worked to find for it
an independent position along with these other two, not
hostile to them but beholden to neither, from which it
could strive freely with them for the spread of Christ's
Kingdom. Though they reasoned cogently, it would perhaps be premature to assume that the independence of the
university and a fitting place for the teacher were then
established for all time.

The theoretical justification for the new kind of community of learning, or Republic of Letters, within the
larger community of men had been slowly and painstak-
ingly spelled out over a period of more than a thousand
years. The effort began with the early Church Fathers; it
was continued and strengthened by the learned monks,
and later still by the teaching clergy, who lived and worked
and gave themselves to the new universities in medieval

Europe. One meets many famous names in following Dean
Williams' account of this development, from Origen and
Jerome through Alcuin, St. Anselm, and Abelard to Calvin
and thence to the Mathers in Massachusetts. For the Mathers, seventeenth-century Harvard, like Paris before it, was
to be prized as "a learned encampment of the militia of
Christ." It was to be seen as the latest link in the transfer
of learning from Israel to Egypt to Athens and so ultimately to New England, and its professors were held to be
followers of Elisha, in direct line of descent from the
Prophets.

Not many professors would be particularly happy to be
told today that they belong in the line of the Prophets.
For the predominant view now is that the university is not
concerned with such airy nothings as prophecies, or with
kingdoms that never were on land or sea. It is concerned
rather—and, we assume, more maturely—with the hard
facts of a very real world. The university is now largely a
secular institution, and its justification is increasingly
sought in the measure of its contribution, in part to the
State, yes; but perhaps now even more to that new colossus
that looms over both Church and State—the great industrial and commercial organization, the provider of our
present power, which involves all of us and draws into itself an increasingly large part of our whole national life.
That the university is involved deeply with this we tend
now rightly to take for granted; and yet at the same time
we occasionally experience a haunting feeling that though
we have done well to escape the apparently unenlightened
and excessive preoccupation of our predecessors for what
we now patronizingly refer to as "moral and spiritual
values," all is not well.

The earliest defenders of the colleges and universities
wanted to keep them independent of Church and State.

The educational institutions, it was claimed, stood for wisdom, and it was proper and necessary, therefore, that they have an equal position along with those other institutions which were the special representatives of power and faith. This claim for the universities was first made in medieval Europe. Later it was reaffirmed here. And yet at Harvard's founding in the seventeenth century its original board of control was made up half of clergy and half of representatives of the State, and it was not at last until the period of the Civil War that she won the right through her own alumni to choose her overseers. This may suggest that it is easier to make a claim than to have it honored. But a more significant consideration for our present purpose is that the oldest American university had its independence officially recognized by the State only as recently as the very eve of the period of development that produced the modern university.

That the university had to be free was clear to the thoughtful from its very inception, for it is only thus that a university can give itself to that pure, disinterested, and unfragmented learning it is its purpose to seek. On the other hand, it was not imagined in medieval Europe or in seventeenth-century New England that the pursuit of learning would be deemed possible outside a context of faith. In these early periods it appears not to have occurred to anyone that *veritas* and *fides* were separable. It was rather simply taken for granted that what the university was pursuing was a combination of reverence and wisdom. It is curious that now, after seventy-five years of a different kind of university, we have returned to a condition where an informed contemporary philosopher of education states the joining of these two things to be our most pressing present need. Robert Ulich says in his new book *The Human Career* that what is most needed in education today is the attitude of "rational piety," or if one prefers it the other way round, as perhaps best suits the university, "devout reasonableness." One further conviction of the early defenders of the university should be set down here. This is their belief that the university community was an armed encampment of the militia of Christ engaged continuously in a special kind of spiritual warfare. This latter fact, if one looks beneath the quaintness of the language, might suggest that the university as envisaged by our ancestors was not so unconcerned about the actualities of this world as has sometimes been supposed.

Today we still want—and rightly—to keep the universities independent of Church and State. But there is now in America, as I have suggested, a new, huge, mundane entity that has perhaps become even more dangerous for higher learning than either of these. This is the world without spirit, the world of the ordinary—the circumscribed, narrowly material world of men which drains most of our energies into its service and will not, unless it is made to do so, yield final meaning beyond its own superficial self. The greatest present threat to the free, disinterested, and lively play of mind, and to that shoring up and direction of mind that must always come from faith, seems to come not from Church or State but rather from those other demanding, dominant forces and concerns—largely economic—that now run rampant, threaten to drive out spirit, and almost engulf our daily life.

It was said some time ago that "salvation by the acquisition and application of knowledge is on the way to becoming the religion of modern man." This "religion" has tended increasingly to place its trust in applied knowledge. The readiness of the university to serve this aim was greatly accelerated during World War II. It has since continued unabated, and many, both within and without the university—many who love universities most dearly and who wish with all their heart to labor in their service— now encourage them zealously to move further and faster in this direction. So the university's attention and strength are drawn increasingly into the service of practice. And this at a time when at long last—and most commendably —industry is beginning to pay more of the bill for higher education.

In an earlier period it was necessary to point out the threat to the university presented by both Church and State, and to develop a theoretical justification that would keep it free from the control of either. We have been well alerted to these dangers. But is it not time now to hammer out a fresh justification for the university in modern society that will give it a new sense of direction, and at the same time to save it from excessive preoccupation with the ordinary in life and from idolatrous service of economic activity?

Richard Hofstadter in his essay "The Development of Higher Education in America" says, "If one had to single out the one feature of the American climate that has been most unfortunate for higher education, it would probably be the implicit assumption that education is something that ought to pay its way, that it is an instrumentality rather than one of the goals of life, that it must justify itself by providing a quid pro quo." Now as the conception of the function of education becomes increasingly circumscribed, the danger in this assumption grows. It is perhaps possible that a new kind of serfdom for universities lies not far ahead.

It is in crying out against this danger—the ever-present danger of succumbing to the illiberal and the spiritless in human life—that Henry Wriston, as a leader in education for more than thirty years, has shown himself to be in the direct line of the Prophets. It has been his mission again and again to point out that, though by restricting the range of our interest we can drive rapidly toward a limited goal, too little is gained when this is done by beating down the finer reaches of the human spirit. For he has known and has helped us all to see that where concentration on a narrow worldly objective takes over, color and enhancement and finally meaning depart from life to leave grayness, repetitiveness, and ordinariness to rule there unopposed.

In winding up his activity at Lawrence College preparatory to coming to Brown University as President, Henry Wriston wrote in his book *The Nature of the Liberal College:*

... A liberal education ... is a profound experience ... The effects are not transitory; they are part, thereafter, of ... [one's] personality ... Things which alter life ... most significantly ... are all things the values of which are direct, immediate, subjective, and intrinsic ... [There is a] fundamental yearning [in people] for a glimpse at the reality and the significance of life ... [The] enormous market for the bogus wares ... [which one sees in the mundane world] is only the margin of the real market. Those who achieve health and those who attain a liberal education do not patronize these frauds ... [The quest for understanding] must be a life-long preoccupation ... We live in an age of engineering ... Vocational training and even professional training have some remote analogies to engineering, but liberal education has none ... The philosophic approach to the whole of life is not only just as necessary, but just as practicable, today as in other days ... Distinguished educators have been known to insist that the function of a college is to train the mind, and that other aspects of experience, and specifically the emotions, are irrelevant. The statement does not make sense ... [The environment is hostile to liberal education. The usual business and professional environment is almost disastrous. But] the

liberal ideal—that freedom of the mind and spirit from fear
and all inhibiting emotions—is particularly valuable in a
world enslaved to lesser objectives . . . [If the undergraduate
student] is making a man of himself, he is doing the world's
most important job . . . Growing and working, thinking and
gaining power, reflecting and gathering insights, the student
justifies his life; the future may safely be left to its own devices.

This is in the great tradition of higher education. There
has been much talk in recent years that education consists
in adjustment, of individuals to groups and of universities
to the changing condition of society. The word "adjustment" in this sense would not sit very well with Mr.
Wriston. He would, rather, agree completely, as every
act of his life has always demonstrated agreement, with
another recent statement by Robert Ulich that "only a
slave adjusts to every situation; a free man knows when
to say yes, or no."

Universities were not put into the world to play the
servile role of administering exclusively to ordinary mundane needs. It may be that in seeking to escape such dis-
honor they have sometimes withdrawn into a too-detached
position. But today the danger is clearly from the other
direction. There is new need to recognize that though
universities have a concern and a responsibility toward the
everyday world their primary, their fundamental, responsibility lies totally elsewhere. This is for basic investigation, for the pursuit of learning almost for learning's own
sake, for poetry and for vision, and then from this kind of
experience for the provision within society of a critically
constructive force. And this is the kind of activity that
communities should respect in, and indeed demand from,
their universities. However high our opinion of ourselves,
universities are not the creatures of modern industrial
society. Nor should they be enslaved to that society. They

spring rather from an ancient, broad, and deep tradition of mind and spirit. Nurtured in adventure, boldness, and fresh vision, they have always recognized at their best that their responsibility is not to minister to utility but rather to call men to moral and spiritual, and to intellectual, responsibility. It is only thus that they can ever hope to serve the real needs of society.

The present chief danger for a college or university is then that, from preoccupation with business life, or from fatigue, or from a lack of grasp on what the spirit means for life, it will yield to the pressures that are always working to make it conform itself to the world—not at the world's novel, creative best, but at its less thoughtful, almost meaningless ordinary. Thus it is possible for a university without being aware of it to slip into a servile relationship with the culture in which it finds itself and so betray its real reason for being. This danger as it now presents itself to us in a new form is apt to grow as colleges and universities look increasingly to government and business for the sustenance they must have to keep alive. Limited dependence of this kind need not necessarily be harmful, but it cannot fail to be dangerous if there is not a clear, prior recognition of the way universities deeply and truly serve society. For if the university does not stand as in some sense a critic of society and a force always calling for fresh endeavor, it cannot be the university.

* * * * * * *

JUSTICE, THE UNIVERSITY,
AND THE PROFESSIONS

THE SUBJECT under consideration during this convocation has been government under law. The discussion quite properly was not narrowly confined, but frequently encompassed a variety of problems and considerations sometimes only distantly related to the theme. Yet never has the conversation moved far from the question of justice in the affairs of men, and the responsibility implicit in law, and imposed on all who work with the law, to endeavor to serve this end. Perhaps, therefore, the more inclusive theme of the conference has been justice. If so, the talk we have been having here is only one more chapter in a discussion that has been going on for a very long time.

Without going back to a more distant antiquity, we can find a proximate beginning of this conversation near the very headwaters of western literature in an indignant cry made long ago by a peasant farmer against what he called the "crooked judgments" of certain "gift-devouring princes." Thus early in our western tradition, we meet an appeal from horrendous fact to moral law with a refusal to concur in a situation simply because it is, or to bow with-

Address at the John Marshall Bicentennial Dinner in Memorial Hall, Cambridge, September 24, 1955, concluding the two-day international convocation in Chief Justice Marshall's honor, sponsored by the Harvard Law School.

out protest before obvious injustice simply because of the
strength of the party committing it. Ever since, although
force has never abated her insistence, there have always
been some ready to stand with Hesiod, unwilling like him
to accept as wisdom the hawk's statement to the nightingale that "he is a fool who tries to withstand the stronger."
If there is any one thing deeply rooted in western civilization it is this tradition of moral protest against the unjust
and inconsiderate use of strength.

Another example will underscore the early origin of
this enduring concern for justice. You will remember
reading of that afternoon more than two thousand years
ago when he who has long been a symbol in the west of the
thinking man, and so of the use of reason and analysis in
human affairs, was stopped as he was hurrying away from
the Piraeus to make his way back to his own city. He had
gone down to the harbor town earlier in the day to participate in a religious observance. His duty done, he
wanted to go home, but was overtaken and then persuaded
—persuaded, not forced despite a playful threat of force—
to remain for dinner and to see a torch race in the evening.
Scarcely had he arrived at the house of Cephalus, however, when he found himself involved in a discussion that
has never since ceased to intrigue and instruct our western world. Called upon to explain what justice is, and its
power among men, he embarked upon a discussion that
must have lasted for hours even if only a small part of
what is recorded was actually said.

It is a tribute to the importance of the subject that the
discussion of that evening is still going on. Socrates went
a long way round in trying to demolish the heretical view,
stated as forcibly then perhaps as it has ever been stated,
that the word justice is an excessively high abstraction virtually devoid of meaning, having almost no correspond-

ence with any actuality. Socrates wanted to show both that justice *is*, and that it is to be chosen. But in the end, you will recall, he could do no more perhaps than affirm that there is a pattern of it laid up in heaven for the guidance of him who wants it.

At the end of that very long evening (it is doubtful that they ever got to the torch race!) Socrates could do no more than assert that justice exists and has a place in the affairs of men. Perhaps at the end of our three days of discussion we have done no better. But if this is true, it is also true that we have done no less. For there have been few speeches made here during the past few days that have failed to make appeal to moral principle. Implicit in virtually everything said has been a conviction that in most human affairs there is a right as well as a wrong way. The late Mr. Justice Jackson maintained in the Godkin Lectures he was to have given at Harvard in the spring of 1955 that the safety of the juridical order depends in the last analysis upon an informed and committed citizenry—both informed and committed, but no less committed than informed. If this be true, then from the evidence given here, it is clear there is still much of this kind of preservative for free institutions in our country and in the West. We are not yet ready to tailor our values to accord with men and events.

Through the discussion of these days there has repeatedly shone an allegiance to a large number of political and moral principles. Basic to the whole discussion has been the tenet that government exists for the sake of the individual, and that there is a limit to what government can do to him. It seems to have been pretty generally agreed that human affairs must be guided by a sense of decency and fair play, that personality is more to be regarded than property, that men are morally obligated to try to be rea-

sonable and to be guided by reason. There have been repeated references to "fundamental notions of fairness and
justice" and to "the precepts of reason and good conscience." We have been reminded again and again of the
worth and importance of the individual, and we have been
told, correctly, that this was a religious insight before it
became a political aim. There seems to have been an almost universal recognition that though we have only very
imperfect scales to weigh values of this kind in specific situations, the values themselves and, back of them, the age-
long concern for justice, are not to be gainsaid. From
words spoken here, it would appear rather that we are still
committed with Socrates to the view that the word justice
can have meaning, that it stands for something independent of force, that it is desirable for men, and that both
law and government exist to foster its realization.

The fourth century before Christ and the nineteenth
century A.D. were not the only times in history when
analysis laid bare the hypocrisy that can inevitably be
found beneath many human pretensions to virtue and
thus cast doubt upon virtue itself. For almost a hundred
years some of the more searching currents in the thinking
of the western world worked to make it increasingly difficult to keep a grasp on principle. This produced in an
important segment of the population, including large
numbers of those within the universities and in the professions, a deep aversion to discussion of moral principles
—an aversion strengthened by the too-ready proclivity of
indiscriminating individuals to appeal without conviction to principle or to seem to understand without ever
getting near the root of a matter. The efficacy of principle
is brought into question by many less amiable than the old
Scottish preacher whose practice was to extricate himself
from treacherous discussion with his parishioners with the

statement: "It may not be right, and it may not be just, but it is the will of God." If only the will of God could be so certainly known!

If the debilitating prejudice against admitting considerations of principle is now abating, a reason is not far to seek. There have always been some to maintain that the world of knowledge owes little to events. Yet surely it is the events of our century that have been forcing this particular change in intellectual convention. The wars and inventions of this century, with its acts of inhumanity and cynical misuse of elements in our civilized tradition, have quickened fresh interest in the nature and authority of principles long voiced only by rote, whose existence was all too recently either denied or casually and indifferently taken for granted.

In a recent conversation, the Principal of the University of Aberdeen told me happily about a statement of a former teacher of his—obviously a more perceptive Scot than the preacher just quoted—to the effect that "a long look in the dark is worth any number of your penny candles."

We have been having such a long look in the dark at the acts of violence within and among nations of our time that lines are again beginning to be drawn distinctly between those for whom, as another has said, "all law is 'what the Sovereign commands'" and those who "recognize some kind of superior 'Law' that is binding because it is *intrinsically right* and *reasonable.*"

This surely is gain. But have we then only to rejoice? Quite clearly the justification for this and similar conferences is not simply to reaffirm allegiance to principle in the abstract, and to moral order, welcome as this is as a refreshing change. It is rather to suggest a responsibility, again and always, to inquire how principles work in particular instances and how they are constantly to be used and defended. Our proper concern is not justice in the abstract, but the workaday practice of justice. The purpose of such a meeting as this, then, is to give us a fresh view of the goal and encourage us to go to work. And there is need for new effort.

For it is not only people in the universities and professions who have been showing a reawakened interest in our moral and political tradition. Many from various parts of society have in recent years been increasingly ready to make professions of principle and eager to come forward to protect and defend what they take to be our best tradition. A few have done this for transparently dishonest reasons, not because they know or care about the tradition, but because they find it a useful tool. But the great majority clearly have acted in good faith. They do care about the country and its traditions. They want to serve and protect their heritage. Many of these are apt to do so in a crude, uninformed, and destructive fashion. You can cite your own examples. A moral resurgence may be evident in their acts, but it is more to the point that the great majority of them give added testimony that moral intent must ever be shored up with a vast amount of understanding and knowledge if good rather than harm is to result. Our moral convictions may antecede examination, discussion, and debate, but it is also true that it is only as they are raised from obscurantism by examination, discussion, and debate that they rightly and safely become operative in human affairs.

Recently there has been an extraordinary amount of vociferous talk calculated to return our attention to the central truths of our political inheritance. But in too many instances have not these efforts been so ill informed that the tradition carelessly held up by well-meaning people for enforced admiration could not fail to present

itself to many as a miserable caricature of the real thing?
And the end is not yet. There was a peculiarly unpleasant
instance only a few days ago. I refer to what must have
seemed to many an incredibly misguided attack on the
Fund for the Republic and its much maligned president.*

This Fund, as you know, was set up in order that there
be an institution among us to devote single-minded attention to our political inheritance and especially to the preservation of our liberties. Several of the trustees of this
Fund are here tonight. Their program was launched with
this statement: "Basic to human welfare is general acceptance of the dignity of man. This rests on the conviction
that man is endowed with certain unalienable rights and
must be regarded as an end in himself, not as a cog in the
mechanism of society or a mere means to some social end."
There is more in the same vein. As a statement by which
they were to be guided, it had been laid down as early as
1950 that "The Foundation [will] support activities directed toward the elimination of restrictions on freedom
of thought, inquiry, and expression in the United States,
and the development of policies and procedures best
adapted to protect these rights in the face of persistent
international tension." The record should show to any
fair-minded observer that in more than two years of operation the Fund has hewed to this aim.

And yet what happens? Its efforts are denounced in the
public press as un-American by the leader of another

* For nearly a year prior to the delivery of this address the role of American philanthropic foundations had been the object of much political
discussion, and a special committee of the United States House of Representatives had been set up to determine whether these tax-exempt organizations had been subject to subversive influences. The particular attack to
which Mr. Pusey alludes came from the commander of the American
Legion, who urged Legionnaires to shun the Fund and its works on the
ground that it was minimizing the danger of communism and thereby
imperiling national security.

group which is also professedly seeking to serve the country's best interest. *Sunt lacrimae rerum.* It would of course be foolhardy in view of evidence repeatedly brought forth—most recently, for example, in the findings of the Australian Royal Commission on Espionage*—to close our eyes to the very real danger of Communist infiltration. But does not this kind of unwarranted attack from the inside prove also that we are under urgent necessity to be saved from ill-formed, unqualified protectors, and does it not establish beyond cavil the need for the Fund's effort?

There are other examples of the same kind of misguided zeal where violence is done to such central articles in our tradition as respect for evidence and fair play. The several instances when attempts have been made to eradicate all mention of the United Nations from the curricula of public schools belong in this category. Surely obscurantism is not an article in the American creed. And there are other sadly familiar efforts motivated by a runaway desire to achieve security.

The chief trouble with most assertions of principle is that they lead very quickly to self-righteousness. Our feelings get involved, then out the window goes reason. We are right, and the other fellow a fool or a hypocrite. Unfortunately sometimes he is! The final judgment must be left to the Lord. Meanwhile, however, it is necessary to remember that it is the peculiar mission of the university, and of all professions which have their nurturing roots

* As in the United States, the public concern in Australia in 1954–55 regarding the extent of Russian subversion in civic life became entangled in politics. At the time President Pusey spoke, the Royal Commission had just issued a report as a result of its inquiry into the case of Vladimir Mikhailovich Petrov, Third Secretary of the USSR Embassy, who had sought political asylum in Australia. The Commission's allegations became a subject of sharp debate in the Menzies' government's campaign for re-election.

within the university, to believe in principle, yes—but also to have the skill, the knowledge, and the will to work for increased understanding and the resolution of conflict. We cannot—we must not—plead indifference or retire from the field simply because the matter is difficult and feelings run high.

It is of course true that in virtually any issue of moment different people will see the path of principle leading in different directions. This is as unfortunate as it appears to be inevitable, and it makes the matter of determining exactly what principle says in a particular instance most difficult. But it does not destroy the validity of principle or the necessity for new effort. There is a responsibility upon the members of a profession to keep on trying.

It has been said of tradition in literature that it does not consist "in preserving a form or set of forms, but in keeping alive an interest in the solution of contemporary problems in contemporary terms or materials." If in this statement the phrase "contemporary terms" be understood to include the grand precepts of the juridical order we have inherited, then surely the same can also be said of government and law.

It is because of this that certain recent examples of activity in the great tradition, where knowledge and devotion to principle have worked together, can bring encouragement to us all. Not every case has been abandoned to the ignorantly insistent. Here in our own community, for example, Professor Sutherland and his colleagues have worked quietly to throw light on the activity of the Communists in America by making available a digest of the principal judicial and administrative hearings in which the Communist party has been involved. Professor Stouffer has produced his book *Communism, Conformity and Civil Liberties*. In volume after volume the real thing as it operates in Russia has been studied and explained to the American public by various people on the staff of the Russian Research Center. Above all perhaps should be cited the example of the Dean of the Harvard Law School, who with his colleagues, in the difficult matter of the use of the Fifth Amendment, in a time of such emotional tension that reason was all but stifled in parlor, office, and club, sought conscientiously and courageously to bring information to bear. The dictate of prudence, in times such as those through which we have come, is to say nothing. Painfully difficult on the other hand is the exercise of professional responsibility. Under its compulsion one is bid not to seek refuge in silence and thus avoid censure, but to stand for principle, to work for understanding, and, while avoiding self-righteousness, to strive to help people to rational judgment, with full awareness of as broad a range of relevancies as possible, despite the difficulties of the situation. In the eyes of this university, the professional conduct of the Dean and his colleagues has been of a very high order. Knowledge, commitment, courage—all three make part of the professional life, and all three must be involved in our efforts.

A perceptive literary critic said recently that "the problem of the modern literary artist . . . is . . . to find ways of handling knowledge in a context of value." I have been trying to suggest that this is also the problem that confronts teachers and lawyers. Conditions for its favorable solution may be better now than they have been for a long time. There seems indeed to be freshening interest in considerations of value and new hope in the possibility of their realization. Technical knowledge adequate for new endeavor is abundantly at hand, and there will be more of it. It is to be hoped, beyond this, that a time has now come when we can move forward in a new creative effort to understand and practice what is best in our tradition, sacrificing nothing in devotion to reason or allegiance to faith.

John Marshall, I have been told, was a very conservative kind of fellow, and yet surely he was no reactionary. He said in a letter to Charles Mercer in 1827 that the best that can be done for the mass of the people is to educate them. This responsibility lies especially on us in the matter of civil liberties, in the proper sphere of government, and all the rest. In the same letter he went on to say, "But as our country fills up how shall we escape the evils which have followed a dense population?" This is the great problem that now lies before us. We are thus reminded by Marshall's words of the requirements of mind and heart and will that are necessary if we are to continue to move toward the more perfect justice which man has been seeking at least since the time of Hesiod.

The tradition in which we work and which we are called to serve is primarily and inalienably intellectual and experimental. But it is also moral. It envisages a mind working with dedication and direction. It is to be hoped that our meeting will have served to call us all to renewed confidence in this faith.

* * * * * * *

COLONEL WILLIAMS' LEGACY

WE ARE TODAY at a point where many thoughtful
people are speaking out against further expansion of
higher education in America. A very blunt statement to
this end was made the other day by the chairman of the
New York State White House Conference, Mr. Kenneth
Royall, who is a former Secretary of the Army. He stated
without equivocation that there are too many young people in college. Many who have examined the question
more carefully and sympathetically than he share this
view, which has wide support in America and seems to be
accepted almost as axiomatic by most of our friendly
critics overseas. The latter look at least with amusement,
if not with horror or contempt, at what seems to them our
gargantuan collegiate enterprise. Unfortunately, it is not
difficult for them to find evidence to support their unfriendly view: the frittering away and enfeeblement of the
curriculum that has taken place in many colleges and universities, the juvenility and inanity that have invaded
others; and on top of such shortcomings in the program of

Address at a Williams College convocation, October 1, 1955, commem-
orating the 200th anniversary of the death of Colonel Ephraim Williams.
Colonel Williams (1714–1755) was a Massachusetts colonial soldier and
proprietor of Massachusetts lands on the great bend of the Hoosac River
and in the "West Township," now Williamstown. He was killed by the
French in an ambush near the southern tip of Lake George on September
8, 1755, less than eight weeks after having made a will leaving a major
part of his estate to establish a free school in his township. This school
was eventually chartered in 1793 as Williams College.

formal education, the frivolity and divertissement that
have at times, in some places, come too deeply to characterize undergraduate life. There is the additional fact
that older people in industry, in government, in the graduate and professional schools, and in whatever other places
college graduates go, encounter individuals from time to
time who do small credit to their early training. But,
despite this kind of evidence, the assertion that there are
too many young people in our colleges seems to me to be
both futile and wrong.

I shall not base my argument on what seems to be
demonstrable fact that there are many qualified young
people who do not now go on to college. It is, of course,
possible that their numbers are fewer than those college
students who, despite every encouragement, continue to
make too little use of their opportunity. But there is one
argument that has not been properly brought forward
which seems to me decisive. It is an argument which de-
rives from the character of our society itself.

Since long before the founding of Williams College—
the development can be carried back to the time of Harvard's founding—the road to professional advancement
and economic advantage in this country has come increasingly to lead through colleges. This is not why the colleges
have existed; it does not provide a full or a wholly acceptable account of their purpose. But it would be hypocritical
of us were we not to acknowledge this truth. All along,
and more now than ever, attendance at college has opened
the way to rewarding and interesting careers that have not
been so readily open to people who had missed the college
experience. Now it is permissible to say this has been overdone, that the college's help was never and is not now so
indispensable that people cannot get on quite well in our
complex world without it. This is to some extent perfectly

true. But it is also true that the demand in our society for people coming out of the colleges has not slackened with the passage of time, and it is to be noted that often those who most deplore the large enrollments of the present—and the much larger enrollments which threaten our colleges in the future—are as eager as any to attract more college graduates into their own professional or business groups. One hears everywhere of shortages. There are too few engineers, too few people entering the basic sciences, too few college graduates available for government service, too few doctors, too few ministers; above all, too few teachers. And this comes at a time when more families can think of sending their children to college than ever before.

The standard of living, now much the highest we have ever known, keeps on creeping upward. As this happens, more and more parents come to see what college has done to help other people's children. In such a time are they not going to insist, as parents, that their children too shall have this advantage? Of course they are. It is for these reasons—the insatiable demands for highly trained people that grow in an expanding technological society, and the ancient American urge in parents to help their children to go up the socio-economic ladder—that any idea that we can cut back or hold static the numbers of young people going to college seems to me wholly illusory. The one question remaining for profitable discussion—and one about which we might do something—turns rather on the kinds of colleges, or the quality of the colleges, which the increased numbers are going to attend.

When we begin to look at the problem this way, we discover a more constructive basis for criticism about recent, current, and prospective educational practice. We may say that there are too many young people in the colleges when perhaps what we mean is that the colleges do not seem to speak to young people as effectively as they might. This is not quite the same thing. Nor is this owing, at least not owing irremediably, to the numbers of students. Is it not just as fair to state it the other way round and say that our troubles arise not because there are too many students but because there are too few outstanding teachers?

Of course there will be those who immediately counter that this will always be true. But even if one concedes the point, the fact remains that we see quite clearly where a new effort must be made.

Ephraim Williams and all his kind were right in their conviction concerning the importance of education and in their hope that education could be made widely available in order that its fruits and power be generally diffused. We Americans remain almost innocently addicted to this faith. We are not going to surrender it within any foreseeable time. What then are the implications of this education for our New England colleges? It seems to me we should begin by recognizing realistically that we shall probably continue to grow, at least slowly, in the years ahead, as we have in the past, under the pressure of increased population. Also we should hope, despite the formidable difficulty of such undertakings, that there will come in time to be more colleges like Williams and Harvard. It seems to me we should welcome this possibility— welcome it, and go right on working for quality in education. For it is not by turning away from the vitalities of the national development that we shall preserve that especial excellence which we have long believed characteristic of New England colleges, but rather by making a new effort to increase the numbers of first-rate college teachers.

We can frankly admit that the future of the independent colleges of liberal arts is threatened from several sides. They need more money than seems to be immediately forthcoming. Having lived through several periods of dearth, they are now about to be swamped by more students than they want or can see at the moment how to handle. Their plants are inadequate for the increased demands about to be put upon them. More significantly, there is too little and too imperfect popular understanding of their true purpose, or what makes them truly good. But when all this is said, it remains true that the most serious threat comes from the awful possibility that in succeeding generations there may be too few of the kind of teacher who made the American liberal arts college something worth maintaining and extending.

The world of education at every level is filled with countless serious shortcomings, many due to inadequate facilities and a long list of such things. But cutting deeper than any of such finally superficial explanations are limitations in the teaching enterprise itself. Limitation of numbers, yes, and of individual capacity; but also, and more seriously, limitations in the conception of what the teacher can do.

Too many of the hours spent in school at all levels are inordinately and inexcusably empty and dreary. I do not wish to seem to be suggesting that it is the function of the classroom to provide entertainment. But when the classroom has no reach into a wider and deeper meaning than itself and so carries little or no excitement from illumination, then this is lamentable indeed. Education begins to do its full work only when the materials of learning, ably and imaginatively presented, penetrate into the very marrow of the learner and set up there a process of desiring that will not be stilled. When the impact of the thing learned, bursting into the self and filling it with excited awareness of the far-reaching implications in the thing studied, engenders a thrilling realization that the self really matters, and urges on irresistibly to new effort, education of the deepest kind is taking place. It is the awesome power of the great teacher, who must himself have had such experience, to work this kind of magic. But within limitations of degree all teachers are under responsibility to ensure that there be a minimum of what Whitehead called inertness in the transmission of ideas.

The story about Mark Hopkins that has worked so deeply into our folklore has a very great weakness, for it tends to focus attention on the log.* Thus it can be used quite improperly, for example, by those who see no need for new school buildings. But the matters of consequence to which the story should call attention are first of all the quality of Hopkins' mind, and second, the response that such intellectual force draws from a young mind.

Arthur Latham Perry felt this power. He stated it quite simply thus in his diary: "Dr. Hopkins is a *princely mind*." And then he went to the very nub of what must have been Hopkins' power, as teachers in our better colleges will always agree, when he said, "An inference I draw from the effect his sermons have upon me is that the best way to move the feelings is through Reason. Nothing is so intellectual, so logical as his trains of thought; yet nothing moves me to such a pitch of feeling."

Some will think that at this point I have undercut my own argument; that the burden this conception of his task places on the teacher is more than a teacher can at-

---

* Mark Hopkins (1802–1887) was one of the most famous college teachers of his generation. A graduate of Williams College, A.B. 1824, he practiced medicine for a time and in 1830 returned to Williams as Professor of Moral Philosophy and Rhetoric, a position he held until his death in 1887. He was ordained in the Congregational ministry and served as President of the College from 1836 to 1872. The traditional reference to "Mark Hopkins and the log" is ascribed to James A. Garfield, who is said to have commented in 1871 that "a pine bench, with Mark Hopkins at one end of it and me at the other, is a good enough college for me!"

tain; that there are just too few Mark Hopkinses and always will be. I recognize the force of the objection; but certainly not here, any more than anywhere else, does the fact that our success must be partial take away the justification for effort.

The power of knowledge dispelled from a mind that has both range and direction: there is nothing, and can be nothing, in the whole world of education to take its place. Not every teacher can rise to the level of a Hopkins, but surely we may hope for more teachers who will share his conception of their task. Always there have been some of this kind in our elementary and secondary schools and in our colleges and universities. But this will not excuse us from recognizing that their numbers are now too few. For upon the continuous recruitment of their kind depends the quality of the whole American educational enterprise —especially the future of the four-year college of liberal arts.

It is no secret that the profession does not hold out promise of financial reward. There are few places in American society where the result of selfish material greed has shown itself more hideously than in the relatively depressed condition of the profession of teaching. Did we think clearly, this career would certainly be held to be among the most deserving of all.

These unfortunately are facts one cannot ignore. Yet the need is there. At all levels the teaching profession is calling for more of our ablest college graduates, who have been truly moved by learning, to help to extend its hold in our national life.

Teaching, of course, is not the only field. All of the professions and the full range of callings make legitimate claims. In all of them one can live in devotion to learning and to public service. But if one has the skill, the personal gifts, and the love of the enterprise to become a truly great teacher, he is needed more than ever before.

It would be a sad thing for anyone to come into teaching without the necessary personal gifts or without realizing what it means, or if he were later to feel sorry for himself because of his choice. But if one is hardheaded when he starts, and not easily beaten down as he goes along, there are great satisfactions to be had.

It is fortunate that the modest institution in the West Township found a man of trust like Mark Hopkins to carry out Ephraim Williams' "Pleasure & Desire." A sentence of tribute by Hopkins' biographer would, I hope, have pleased the heroic Colonel. There was a rare simplicity in Hopkins' approach to his pupils. "He sought to train them to think their way into the heart of things, and to think in such a fashion that life would have meaning and that they could use their powers to the best advantage."

The inspired and inspiring teacher who knows what he is called upon to talk about, and knows it deeply, is still the great desideratum. The New England colleges have shown special tenacity in clinging to this faith. Our need today is to convert this age-old persistence into a steady stream of able young people who, with the spirited zeal of a pioneer like Colonel Williams, will homestead our contemporary educational frontier and keep alive and extend the faith.

* * * * * * *

EDUCATION AND MEDICINE

An occasion such as this causes a lifting of the heart throughout the whole community, and not least within Harvard University. The history and growth of the University and of many of the Boston hospitals have long been intertwined, and a step ahead for one of them is a step ahead for all. We are especially exhilarated when the step ahead is as considerable as this one has been.

It is a happy coincidence that the Children's Hospital was founded, if I am informed correctly, on January 23, 1869, just a few months before Charles W. Eliot was chosen to be the twenty-first president of Harvard. The prime mover in its establishment was Dr. Francis H. Brown, a graduate of Harvard College in the Class of 1857 and of the Harvard Medical School in 1861, another of those many graduates of Harvard who shared in the founding and developing of hospitals in Boston and in the whole progress of medicine here.

Sometime between 1869 and the present, Harvard became a university—as President Hill, Mr. Eliot's immediate predecessor, had hoped it would become—"in fact as well as in name." During the same period the Harvard Medical School grew to be one of the foremost centers for medical education in this country and the world. And at

_____

Address at the dedication of the new consolidated building of the Children's and Infants' Hospitals, Boston, October 5, 1956.

the same time there occurred major developments in the number and quality of Boston's hospitals.

It is not widely realized that before 1869 there was no university in this country in the sense in which this word is now understood. It is perhaps better known that the imperfect medical education of the earlier time underwent radical transformation during the decades after 1870, as did indeed the care of patients. So recent were the fundamental changes now taken for granted on which the progress of medicine in this community was to depend.

In a sense the advance was started by President Eliot. He taught mathematics and chemistry at Harvard for some seven or eight years after his graduation in 1853. In the early 1860's he resigned from the faculty and went abroad. There he came face to face with the exciting intellectual developments which were creating the great modern continental universities of France, Germany, and Austria. More important for our purpose, he awakened to the realization that what then passed for the higher learning in America had in it a large element of pretense, and that American understanding concerning the range and potential of science was seriously outmoded. Mr. Eliot was excited to discover that European scholarship and research had a reach and depth which most people in the colleges at home had not even begun to suspect to be possible. He seems then in the face of this discovery to have resolved that energy, money, insight and purpose should be marshaled at once to bring America, or at least to bring Boston and Cambridge, abreast of the exciting new developments he had seen abroad.

Mr. Eliot returned to the United States first to accept appointment on the faculty of the newly founded Massachusetts Institute of Technology and shortly thereafter to be chosen Harvard's president. Immediately he and his associates began to build a university and, in the process, to make over professional education, including medical education, in America.

In his very first annual report, given when the Children's Hospital, then situated at 9 Rutland Street in Boston, was only a few months old, Mr. Eliot said, "The whole system of medical education in this country needs reformation." It was his conviction that the teaching of medicine had to be taken away from proprietary schools wedded to practice, and strongly implanted in universities. It was also necessary that it be joined to clinical teaching in hospitals. It had to become a full-time demanding occupation for both students and teachers. A course of lectures given during a few months as a supplement to apprentice training could no longer be considered adequate preparation. The study of medicine was to be rooted in laboratories, libraries, and hospitals and carried on continuously and progressively over a period of years. It must recruit abler and better prepared teachers and students. And it must be endlessly concerned, as was the whole University, to advance knowledge.

President Eliot and those who cared about the progress of medicine in his generation were convinced of the truth of these propositions, and forcefully and imaginatively set about translating them into fact.

It is of course an exaggeration to say that medical education began in Boston only this side of 1869. In actuality it had had a considerable and not undistinguished earlier history. But however much one praises the achievements of the early founders—the first Warrens, Jacksons, Shattucks, and the rest—the dramatic advances of the later years seem virtually to have constituted a new beginning which had been made necessary by the general progress of science. From Mr. Eliot's day, medical education and medicine in Boston have gone on from strength to strength. The magnificent transformation now effected in this hospital devoted to the disease and to the health of children is only the latest chapter in a long and exciting story.

Today the pattern of medical education in America is well established, and it is sufficiently strongly implanted within the structure of the higher learning to seem to be able to resist almost any misconceived effort which might now be made to turn the practice of medicine back into a trade. Medical education is today a mature, carefully articulated discipline of scientific investigation and learning. Its strength, here and elsewhere, springs from the coordinated efforts of many parts. At one end of the process its work goes on in a network of strong, well-equipped, carefully staffed, and imaginatively directed hospitals, such as this one, themselves fully committed to teaching, research, and the advance of medical knowledge as well as to the care of patients. Even the patient is now completely convinced that his care largely depends on the teaching and research which go on in hospitals. At the other end of the process, in almost every center where medicine flourishes today, there is a complex modern university with strong departments in all of the basic sciences and in many other fields which contribute to knowledge of men. These —the hospitals and the university—are the right and left hands of medical education. And between them, joining them, belonging to both, in both, using both, is the medical school itself. Throughout this whole broad institutional sequence the process of seeking, investigating, learning, and teaching goes forward, continuously, if with somewhat different emphases now and then in various of the parts.

Since the time when the elaboration of medical knowledge came under the aegis of the university, the boundaries of the known in the old subjects of medicine have been enormously extended, and almost endless new subdivisions have sprung up. This is the happy result of that advancing specialization which has now been carried on assiduously by competent scholars in many areas in all parts of the world through several generations. It cannot stop. But it presents a serious problem to pedagogy.

It was Archbishop Temple who observed some time ago that a modern university is in danger of becoming "a place where a multitude of studies are conducted, with no relation between them except those of simultaneity and juxtaposition." Insofar as this is true it is a misfortune, inevitable as it may sometimes seem; but when viewed through the student's eyes it could easily become a nightmare, because the student is expected to bring all of the myriad, complex, isolated pieces of his knowledge together into organic, intellectual union.

It is fortunate therefore that experiments to discover better ways of teaching medicine are now being pushed forward, here and elsewhere. Complete answers are still to be found; perhaps never will be wholly found. But the goal is admirable. What is sought today is not the stuffed head, but broad interest and awareness, and with these an informed and inquiring mind.

It is not only the endless differentiation within fields of knowledge and the enormous increments to the known which cause difficulty. Equally formidable is the widening conception of what is relevant in medical education. This has so vastly expanded in recent years that the task confronting teachers of medicine only a few decades ago now seems in retrospect to have been very simple indeed.

The Dean of the Harvard Medical School has said that

"scientific medicine must become comprehensive medicine, and yet not become thereby any less scientific." A
great deal is implied in the phrase "comprehensive medicine." For the viewpoint of medicine, as much concerned
with the localized pathological event as before, has in this
generation been so sharpened and broadened that today it
sees such an event in the context of the whole person, and
the person in his turn within the fullness of environmental
circumstance. The doctor has become more than doctor.
He is doctor and sociologist, scientist and humanist, in-
vestigator, administrator, psychiatrist, wise man, philosopher and friend. And more perhaps than these.

The burden placed upon him and upon the educational
system which must produce him is now immense. Having
started with a relatively restricted view of its task, medical
education has been persuaded to revise this view by the
success of its own efforts. Since the universities were
founded and advance begun, medicine has in this century
been drawn steadily into wider and wider responsibility:
not only must it help the sick, but it must now go many
steps farther and try to assure conditions of health in the
individual, the family, the community—and, beyond
them, the whole world.

This is the breath-taking vision to which the science of
medicine has now attained. I confess that when I hear it
expounded by those best informed and most persuaded
that such achievements are within reach I sometimes feel
there is something here of what the Greeks called *hybris*,
that overweening pride in man which seems wantonly to
invite trouble. Yet if a question be raised as to whether
medicine should accept such a challenge, we have no al-
ternative but to answer, "Why yes, of course. It must."

Dean Berry has said that good medical education is
nothing more nor less than good education. By inference

Dean Berry is declaring that the most serious problems confronting medical education are not essentially different from those confronting the whole of higher education. Of first importance is the necessity to keep the conception of purpose clear and high. Not only in medicine—but as much here as anywhere—there is an unremitting threat to good education arising from too great willingness to compromise with the immediate urgencies of practice. Substantial advance will not come from excessive concession at this point. Next there is continuing need both to recruit talent and to elicit in individuals a will to learn and to keep on learning. It is also essential in every generation that there be a continual renewal of the numbers of those teacher-learners of ability whose lives are lived on the frontiers of their subjects. There are also practical pedagogical problems: How most effectively to handle increasing masses of information? And more difficult: How to achieve wholeness of understanding in the face of the fantastic growth of the amount to be known? Individuals, whole faculties in many provinces of the higher learning, are now wrestling earnestly with such questions as these.

And there are questions of another kind confronting education in medicine: How to deepen the sense of professional responsibility? How to organize a system of education which will produce increments not only in what a man knows but also in what he is? And there are problems at an even deeper level. How in an increasingly depersonalized world to teach a man to hold tight to a sense of individual human significance and to continue to care for people? Perhaps the greatest responsibility confronting all education in the end is so to ground the process in understanding and imagination that it will lead on toward a good society and not into Orwellian nightmare.

Here in this city, in this part of the world, medical

education has had an extraordinary growth and exhilarating achievement. We find a proximate beginning for this activity in the curiosity of a group of eighteenth-century Harvard undergraduates who long ago organized an anatomical society secretly to dissect cats and dogs. The requisite mental quality and a will to understand and to advance knowledge were already present in them. It is not surprising that it was one of these young men who saw the need and established Harvard's first program of medical education founded on systematic instruction and clinical experience.

Much has flowed from this modest beginning. Today the program of instruction in medicine in Boston, and elsewhere, draws strength from a vast network of laboratories, departments, schools, and hospitals joined together for the care of patients, for the continuation and advance of medical knowledge, and for the positive promotion of health.

It is worth emphasizing that the first large flowering of this array of medical resource came almost half a century ago, that in a sense we have for a long time been living in no small measure on the capital of an earlier generation. Almost all that was new then has since shown signs of wear, in some instances even of decay. This is true not only in Boston but in other medical centers as well. Fortunately, the process of rebuilding is now under way. First-rate medical education, on which, in the long run, first-rate medical care must depend, needs first-rate facilities as well as first-rate men to do its work. So too does first-rate care for patients. What has been achieved here in this effort of rebuilding and modernization at the Children's Hospital is an exemplary achievement, one which must point a way for many of the rest of us.

Boston medicine has been brought through the efforts

of many to a position of enormous power and respect. It has very great resources and an inspiriting tradition. But its very success and brilliance draw it constantly into wider and wider responsibility and so into greater need. No one would want this to be otherwise, or would want now to turn back. The promise is too great.

All units in the empire of medicine in Boston can rejoice in the increased strength which has come to the Children's Hospital. They can be confident that generations of patients and of those who care for them—doctors, nurses, students, teachers—will be grateful to the thoughtful and generous multitude who have helped to prepare this hospital for increased usefulness to mankind.

Cletis T. Eskew

* * * * * * *

AN ISLAND OF LIGHT

I CAME to Harvard in the autumn of 1924, an unintimidated freshman in an expectant and receptive mood. My first impression, as I suppose is true of most new students who come to Cambridge from the Midwest, was a sense of the history around me illustrated by Harvard's old buildings and other evidences of a notable past of which I was only vaguely conscious through my reading. But my second impression was of my classmates—or at least the first group of them I met.

The first time I entered the dining hall of Gore, which was then a freshman dormitory, I went to the nearest empty chair. As I sat down, I said hello to my two or three nearest neighbors. They must at least have looked in my direction; perhaps they may well have grunted a response to my greeting, as a minimum concession to etiquette. But my clear recollection is that with very little recognition of my presence they went right on talking animatedly among themselves.

What talk it seemed to be! Shaw, Ibsen, Nietzsche. Back and forth the conversation went, in the clever fragmented sentences of quick repartee. Before dessert they had gone on to Katherine Mansfield, and then in a postprandial few

A reminiscence contributed to the little volume, *College in a Yard: Minutes by Thirty-Nine Harvard Men,* edited by Brooks Atkinson (Cambridge, Harvard University Press, 1957); copyright 1957 by the President and Fellows of Harvard College.

minutes they dealt, to their satisfaction and mine, with Cabell and Mencken.

This was not the kind of talk which experience with contemporaries back home had led me to expect. I was at once amazed, terrified, excited, and pleased. And so began my experience of Harvard.

The names of the authors discussed so confidently at that meal have remained in my memory, for though I may have heard of them before coming to Harvard, I certainly had not read them, and later, as I discovered them for myself, their names were driven into my memory. Each time I met one, I recalled the sick feeling I had had that first night when I came to Harvard alone—my first trip east of Chicago—and was confronted with the incredible, if perhaps—may I add this now?—slightly pretentious erudition of a select new group of Harvard undergraduates clearly much better prepared for what lay ahead than I. But may I also say that the great respect I acquired for Harvard undergraduates at that time, though it may since have changed character, has never been diminished in even slight degree by prolonged association with them?

Dare I admit that now my most vivid recollection of my first year's study is a phrase from a freshman German examination? The teacher of this course was a lively young German graduate student, a superb teacher, whose name, unfortunately, has long since left me. For our final examination in sight reading he had written in German a short, whimsical account of an American movie. Perhaps he had the senior Douglas Fairbanks in mind. At any rate, in the first few sentences the hero was shown performing a series of incredible physical exploits. Next we were shown the heroine in peril, drowning in a mountain lake. As I recall, the text then ran something like this: "But don't worry, it is now nearly eleven o'clock, and since this is a movie all must

soon end happily." At once the hero appeared from nowhere, dove into the lake, thrashed about madly, if osten-
tatiously, and finally pulled the heroine safe to shore.
Immediately the camera came close to reveal her in his
arms, dry, beautiful, and perfectly groomed, and then, at
the end, moved from the handsome, happy couple, to show
a little dog who looked on (the typical movie fade-out of
the period) *"und wedelt mit dem Schwanze."*

I imagine we were supposed to be learning which cases
followed which prepositions, but this particular teacher,
like so many teachers at Harvard, was teaching a great deal
more than the immediate matter in hand. It was his guiding idea, I suppose, that to get on in the world we should
learn to be critical; but it was also salutary for us that in
his practice criticism was always characterized by good
humor.

A year or two later I had found my way into courses of
John Livingston Lowes and Irving Babbitt. From that
time, each day was filled with what were to me fresh ideas
and excited inspiration to read and go on learning. Professor Lowes' course in sixteenth and seventeenth century
lyric poetry was one of the first at Harvard which for me
seemed completely to break through the limitations of the
containing course. It was not so much an exercise in learning as an experience of life itself. There was much in the
course of interest and delight, but what chiefly remains
now is an image of Lowes reading—one might almost say
barking—an endless flood of lyric poetry with such delight
that one could not fail to feel its enchantment.

> It was a lover and his lass,
> With a hey, and a ho, and a hey nonino.

*   *   *

Tell me where is Fancy bred,
Or in the heart or in the head?

*   *   *

If she think not well of me,
What care I how fair she be?

And there is Babbitt, rolling a pencil between his hands,
looking over the tops of his glasses, saying of Tennyson's
Locksley Hall: "This scientific belief in the far-off divine
event is nothing other than a form of nostalgia, an offshoot
of the Romantic imagination, illegitimately associated with
the religious virtue Peace." It was heady stuff for a young
student finding his way into the world of ideas. This and
much more of the kind in endless profusion. Whatever one
thought of Babbitt's point of view, there was never any
mistaking that he had one, nor any reason to doubt that
he was every day dealing with matters of immense and
urgent importance. From him one learned more than ever
that life and learning are not to be separated—that what
one thinks matters! He was a superlative pedagogue whose
classes were full of import, broadly conceived as few would
now dare—and never dull.

The intimate experiences of Harvard are, of course, as
individual and as numerous as the students who come
here. Today it may be that I am more aware of and impressed by the variety and range of intellectual interest
represented in the great faculty of the whole University,
and by the faculty's importance both for enriching the
known and for keeping alive the possibility for learning,
than I am perhaps by students. But fortunately there is no
need to set these two groups against each other. They both
belong; together they make Harvard.

In the complex and confused world in which we all find
ourselves it is possible to think of Harvard as a kind of

island of light in a very widespread darkness, and I must confess I sometimes do just this. But I also know that the figure is not really an apt one, for Harvard has never been an island severed from the broad concerns of men and is certainly not one now. Instead, it is rather intimately involved in the complex culture to which it belongs. Its distinction is that in it intellectual activity has an opportunity to come into sharper focus, and so becomes richer, more vivid, more convincing, and more captivating than in society at large.

As the freshman comes into this place he cannot fail to be impressed by the extraordinary liveliness, concentration, and devotion with which learning long has been and is now pursued—nor can a President!

THE AGE OF THE SCHOLAR

IN THE NINETEENTH CENTURY, the standard to which all questions concerning the higher learning were referred for settlement was the practice of the continental, chiefly the German, universities. Their excellence was beyond challenge. Early in the century a university career held the highest attraction for a considrable portion of the ablest young men of the German states. The scholar enjoyed a standing in the German society of that time such as he has rarely, if ever, attained in any other time or place in history. The achievements of eminent members of these faculties throughout the century were breath-taking in their number, their scope, and their originality. And yet, in the 1890's, when the German universities were in their zenith, their combined faculties numbered only about twenty-five hundred individuals serving a total of thirty thousand students a year.

Today, after eighty years of effort, since the first steps taken by Gilman of Johns Hopkins, Eliot of Harvard, and others, there are in America several-score fully matured universities, each with immense libraries, laboratories, and collections, with faculties numbering in the hundreds if not in the thousands together with scores of thousands of students, and programs of teaching and research which require sums for their annual support many times the size of

---

Address at the eighty-first Commencement exercises of The Johns Hopkins University, Baltimore, June 11, 1957.

the endowments of the universities of eighty years ago. Among our numerous universities there are perhaps a dozen which now take rank with the most fully developed and most effective institutions of higher learning the world has yet seen. Such has been the very considerable increase in the number and quality of universities in America since the time when it was possible to set out to establish a university, as President Gilman did, with a faculty of five or six, a board of trustees, and an endowment of three and a half million dollars.

I am not trying to suggest that intellectual matters are to be judged by quantitative standards. I make these few remarks simply to show how greatly the early efforts to establish universities in this country have prospered, and also to suggest how different has become the situation of the university in a brief period of approximately eighty years. In this century we in America have become an urbanized technological society of unprecedented power, and have created a culture with an insatiable appetite for highly trained men and women in every field of human concern and endeavor, men and women of a kind which only the university can supply. If we have not yet as a people acquired the respect for the scholar which Germans accorded him in the nineteenth century, nevertheless our need for him, it would seem, is now much greater than was theirs.

A few years ago I had occasion to look into the careers of Harvard College graduates in different centuries of our history. In the seventeenth century the vast majority of Harvard graduates became ministers. For example, nine of the eleven members of the Class of 1655 chose this profession, possibly because in the New England village of the seventeenth century the minister was the professional, the educated man, and on him fell a great range of responsibility, both public and private, beyond preaching and pastoral care.

A hundred years later Harvard graduated a class of twenty-five, but only seven of these eighteenth-century Harvard men entered the ministry. The largest single group, nine in number, became lawyers and public officials. By the mid-nineteenth century the graduating class was ninety-two in number. Of this group twenty-four went into business, finance, or manufacturing; twenty-seven became lawyers; ten, only, entered the ministry; and less than a half-dozen continued in education. Is it surprising that President Eliot complained in his inaugural address in 1869 that "it is difficult to find men of the highest distinction for positions in college"? The competition with business and industry, if not with government, was already under way.

In our time, the Harvard College classes contain more than a thousand members at graduation. A considerable number of our recent graduates have been, or are now, involved in military service. But a startling statistic concerning them is that almost three quarters now enroll in some graduate or professional school. Among them are businessmen, doctors, lawyers, teachers, architects, government servants, research chemists—indeed at least a few examples of almost every one of the very many kinds of professionals characteristic of our society, without whom that society cannot now get along.

What I am trying to suggest is that the scholar in America has for some time been growing into a new position of importance and increased influence as our society has developed. I of course use the word scholar here to include more than the research scholar and professor whose career finds its proper setting within the university. It is the academic man, underpaid and neglected as he often is, who remains the most essential scholar; for upon him in the last analysis the whole enterprise of higher learning must depend. But it is proper also now to include within the term many college graduates and almost all of those who have gone on to advanced study in any of the numerous graduate schools or faculties of the university. Through specialized experience of advanced learning such students acquire the ability to make careers, inside or outside the university, in many activities which are now increasingly open only to those who have had, and will continue to have, such experience. For we live in a time of such rapid change and growth in knowledge that only he who is in a fundamental sense a scholar—that is, a person who continues to learn and inquire—can hope to keep pace, let alone play the role of guide. Indeed it is not too much to believe that we may now be coming into an Age of the Scholar, for we have created for ourselves a manner of living in America in which a little learning can no longer serve our needs.

In 1900, one out of sixty young people were graduated from college. In a relatively simple form of society this did well enough. Today our nation has both a more complex society and a new position in the world. One in eight young people now earn college degrees, and many go on to advanced professional study. Since 1940, for example, the number of Ph.D.'s in American society has doubled, increasing at the rate of about 8000 a year. Yet even this increase falls far short of the enlarged and enlarging demand.

The founders of the American university were zealots of a special kind. In a sense, it must be admitted, they were "do-gooders." Impressed by the beauty of high scholarship abroad, they wanted something like it here; but they were never quite at ease with a learning which existed purely for its own sake. It was of the uses of a university that Mr. Gilman and others of his generation normally spoke. Being Americans, they could not help but think of the university as a tool with which to transform society and the world. The result was that from its beginning the university in America has had a peculiarly practical orientation. There has been very little—perhaps too little—of the ivory tower about it.

Because some thoughtful and energetic men could see eighty years ago that the absence of universities was retarding our country's development (as many other peoples of the world have come since to see), doubting Thomases at that time might easily have disputed the asserted need for universities. Today the case is made and the university's importance established beyond cavil. Indeed it is even possible now, because of the widespread and increasing hunger which exists for the graduates of universities, to look forward hopefully to a time when they may well begin to receive the enlarged support they have long both needed and deserved.

The graduating classes which come from the universities each year, the fruits of the very varied research which goes on in them, the materials for study collected, treasured, and kept alive in them: these have become the life-blood of our complicated, developing society; and they have earned a widespread respect for the results of learning if still too little genuine understanding and love for learning itself.

Thus far the best-known achievements of universities have contributed chiefly to health, to longer life, to defense, and above all to a more varied and a more productive economy. Indeed the universities have succeeded so brilliantly at such points that there is now some danger within them lest they become the captives of their success.

Knowledge in the natural sciences, however tentative, has been enormously advanced. Now the social sciences, too, are flourishing and are making increased impact on our common life. But great as they are, the achievements of universities have not yet contributed spectacularly either to strengthen order, or to deepen satisfaction and elicit creativity in individual lives. Power has been immensely increased, but reason's hold upon it is not notably more secure.

Yes indeed, the university in America has acquired strength. After eighty years it is even winning standing in a prestige-serving society. Perhaps this is a sign we should begin now to beware. Could Mr. Gilman and Mr. Eliot, or other founders of their generation, see our universities today, they could not fail to be enormously pleased at how they have multiplied and grown. They would rejoice in their increased utility and in the wide acceptance they have won. But they would be struck, too, I believe, by hopes of theirs that have not been realized, and once they had found their way among us, it is not inconceivable that they might then begin again to raise questions.

They might first say, "How splendid, and how fortunate for you! Yours is the opportunity we were looking to and working for." But would they not then go on to ask, "Since the university has grown to such stature in your time, and has now established its influence so ineradicably everywhere in your society, surely now at long last it can begin more successfully, more powerfully to affect that society for good?" (Their energetic concern for human betterment would not have been diminished by the passage of time.) And then they might ask, "Will it do so? Will it now live up to its high calling and continue to extend the kingdom of mind and spirit in society, or will it rather, forgetting this chief purpose of its founding, take on a more limited view of its function, and be content rather to minister unto power, to multiply jobs (increasingly perhaps, now jobs for machines), and so unwittingly, because of failure of vision and slackened purpose, be a party to a slow dehumanization of men?" Such sombre questions they might address to the university; but what they would really be asking about would not be the university, which is of course an abstraction, but rather about today's scholars and their own motivating conception of their task.

Early in our history Emerson tried to suggest what the American scholar would have to be like. Showing perhaps something of the influence of Carlyle, he cast him in the hero's mold. He defined him as "That man who must take up into himself all the ability of the time, all the contributions of the past, and all the hopes of the future." His language now seems a bit flamboyant, but the responsibility which falls on all of us taken together who today make up the American scholar is surely something like this. Emerson went on to say that the scholar's task is "to cheer, to raise, and to guide men by showing them facts, facts amidst appearances." It was and remains a big order. It is a bigger order now than it was then. But today the scholar is being given a more promising opportunity.

In the first place there are more of us. This commencement season, for example, a third of a million young people will be completing their undergraduate college careers, and scores of thousands more are completing some degree of advanced professional education. The numbers are there. The real question is, what conception of their task and of their responsibility have they acquired? And if it be true that we are indeed moving into an Age of the Scholar, then this large question must be asked: Will all of us taken together respond fully to the great opportunity

now being given to the American university, and to the
American scholar, to enhance the quality of our common
life, and toward this end, will we begin now more aggres-
sively to lead?

Emerson had some early misgivings at this point. The
doubt passed through his mind that when he came the
American scholar might not prove to be the man who was
envisioned and needed. His special fear was lest he be
found wanting in courageous independence, ambition,
and self-reliance. It would not do were he to be a small-
souled person who would settle for little gains or be content like a clansman to rejoice in the glory of a chief. Is
not the principal disgrace in this world, he asked, in speaking of the scholar, "to be reckoned in the gross, in the hundred, or the thousand of the party . . . and our opinion
predicted?" And then this statement, compounded both
of assertion and of prayer, "Not so, brothers and friends—
please God, ours shall not be so." For him, as for Gilman
later, the scholar was to guide.

Now, at long last, events conspire to enhance the scholar's chances. He has not always had the standing of a hero
in our society. Indeed he has tended rather as a rule to be
crowded from the stage, sometimes to be abused. For the
most part he has had to make his way against the current,
with little encouragement, often in loneliness and neglect,
poorly rewarded, enjoying esteem chiefly in the eyes of a
few of like mind. To some degree this is likely in part to
remain true, but because of the vastly enlarged need for
scholars in a technologically advanced society a change is
coming, and the scholar may expect to be looked to in the
future as he has not been in the past.

The university is a community of scholars. Its task is to
know, to study, to care, to guide—to seek to know all that
has been learned and is of concern to men, to keep this

knowledge viable, to have it studied and taught, to add to it—and in so doing, by a myriad of separate efforts to increase mind's influence in the world.

It was an article of faith of those who worked to establish the university in America—of Mr. Eliot, Mr. Gilman and all the others—that all who learned from the university would devote themselves assiduously, hopefully, and joyously, to this great task. So great was the founders' love of and confidence in the beneficent effect of learning, and so great for them its appeal. In a time of immensely increased opportunity such as is now given to us, their successors in the university—when the potential for achievement by the higher learning has been extended far beyond their fondest dreams—surely today our concern, our effort, and our hope can be no less.

* * * * * * *

SECULARISM AND THE
JOY OF BELIEF

IF ALL THE BACCALAUREATE SERMONS which
have been given in Cambridge since 1642 had been pre-
served, one might very well discover reflected in them something of the intellectual history of the western world during
the past three centuries, but I should be very much surprised if there would be much evidence in them of advancing secularization. Their traditional emphasis has always
undoubtedly been strongly religious. In 1864, for example,
Andrew Preston Peabody preached on the subject "The
Christian Order of Nobility." He called for "religious con-
secration of hearts and lives," and said to the Senior Class
of that year that "on you as scholars religion has peculiar
claims." And he could apparently count on being heard
sympathetically and also understood when he added,
"Christian piety alone can give the crowning grace to your
character. If that soul be sensualized, materialized, conver-
sant with earthly things alone, your best intended endeavors for the good of others are limited by the limitations of your own being." Perhaps we can all agree with
my first point, which is simply that times have changed.

The word "secularization" denotes a growing attachment to a way of life in which there is neither need nor
place for religion. It cannot be defined positively simply as

Abbreviated text of the Baccalaureate Sermon for the Senior Class of
Harvard College, Harvard Memorial Church, June 8, 1958.

attachment to or concern for the world of human habita-
tion, for this was and is the prior, characteristic point of
view of various religions, notably Christianity, whose
God, it will be recalled, so loved this world that he gave
His life for it. It has, therefore, rather to be described
negatively as a way of life, which, though its hope like that
of Christianity is in the world, proceeds deliberately
without concern for religion; that is, without any dependence on or need for the concept of God. Indeed, in
occasional instances, it exhibits rather fierce hostility to
this concept.

It may well have been Herbert Spencer who first gave
currency to this meaning of the word. I do not know; but,
whenever the beginning, there can be no question that
secularism is today a powerful force in the world—in the
West as well as in the East. There are many forms and
varieties of it. And wherever it is—even in academic
communities!—it makes traditional forms of worship difficult, because secularism has no need of the traditional
object of worship, which is God.

The understanding or knowing what to do in the face
of this situation is made doubly difficult because up to a
point secularism is indisputably a good thing. The dy-
namism it has unleashed has had a great deal to do with
building the world as we know it. Indeed, so great have
been its successes that it has itself become a faith and
raised a hope that man can through his own efforts—without God—solve all the remaining problems which stand
between him and a secular paradise on earth. Its temples
may be laboratories and factories, perhaps also libraries!
Its very laudable goals are the complete understanding of
the physical universe and the mind of man, and then the
shaping of these after the heart's desire. Individuals have
been swept along in the advance of secularism, and have

become fascinated, if also perplexed, by it. In the confusing, promising, but problem-ridden world it has created, a tragic result has been, as Sir Walter Moberly has
said, "some think God exists, some think not, some think
it is impossible to tell, and the impression grows that it
does not matter."

The chief point I should like to emphasize is simply
that in my opinion it does matter, hard as it is in our
present situation to say this or to have it understood.

There can be no quarrel in a university with secularism
in itself, but only with it as it come hubristically in its
turn to pretend to speak for the whole of life. J. H. Oldham, a British author knowledgeable about both the secular world and the religious, on whom I am dependent for
much of what I am here trying to say, has defined in this
way what is clearly one of the major problems of our time:
"It is one of the many debts which we owe to Baron von
Hügel," he says,

that he cleared up much confused thinking by showing con-
vincingly in his great work, *The Mystical Element in Religion,*
that there are areas or levels in human life that have their
own proper autonomy over against the religious view and are
governed by their own distinctive laws with which religion
has no right to interfere. Religion, he affirmed, is both everything and *not* everything. Christianity not only acknowledges
the rights of the secular, but is especially concerned to affirm
those rights. The scientist must be free to disregard religious
considerations in pursuing his studies in his special field. The
modern world has been right to repudiate ecclesiastical direction in secular affairs. Where Christianity takes issue with the
trend of modern society is the assumption that man's relation
to the objective world is the whole of life.

Mr. Oldham's own chief interest is in religion; his point
is that man's relation to the objective world is not the
whole of life, and that secularism, in so far as it proceeds

on the assumption that it is, falls short, and must always fall short, of adequate ministry to human need. Here is the crux of the difficulty, for at this point, it seems, individuals will simply insist on seeing the same human situation quite differently. For my part I do not know how to make clear what is at stake other than by simply asserting that the questions which are finally of most importance to all of us in our private lives and for the health of our "selves" are not the questions which secular inquiry normally asks of nature, important as these are. They are rather the questions which religion *answers* for her believers by supplying meaning to life, by kindling hope, and by giving through faith in God a basis for ethical behavior. It is because religion does these things for her believers that it is so important; just as it is that as religion does them her truth is validated.

It is fair to ask why a part of life or an attitude toward life which promises so much has among such wide segments of society fallen into disfavor. The attractiveness of secularism supplies part of the answer, but not the whole of it.

The impression of the irrelevance of religion has been mightily strengthened among thoughtful people by the shortcomings they have sometimes observed among those who would advance its cause. Too often, for example, they have found in the churches juvenile conceptions of God, primitive notions of a large-size man who exists to be pleased, like an old-style father, or a stern, perhaps even petulant judge, or at best of some kind of anthropomorphic figure whose conduct could be compared to that of our own more virtuous human beings only to His disadvantage, as Homer's gods with Homer's heroes. It has been my impression that atheists often have in mind some such gods as these, and so it is not surprising, though it is ironical, that in so far as the unbelievers kill them off they undoubtedly also serve the cause of religion.

The churches have failed again and again, at this most central point, to help their people to understand that though God cannot be seen as an object is seen, nor met face to face, He can be felt—if we will let Him enter our lives—as all-pervasive, concerned in all the experiences of life; and He is to be experienced very close to us indeed in every redeemed human relationship. We can be taught not to be afraid or scornful of mystery and to live in trust with the simple fact that a God who can be fully encompassed by our minds cannot really be God.

There have been other shortcomings from the side of religion which have aided the advance of secularism: aesthetic failings, poor music, impossible hymns, unhelpful, moralistic sermons, the mistaken notion that churches are for "good" people rather than for sinners, or that one goes to church as a favor to God; above all, the failure of the churches to rouse themselves, to cease contending among themselves, indeed one might say to "desecularize" themselves, in order to be concerned not for their own selfish interests but, lovingly, for the whole of the world and the whole of life within it. When one considers how inadequately churches have served the needs of people in this new technological and secularly attractive age it is not so surprising that many have withdrawn from or remain outside churches, to the advantage of the growing secularization. It is even more to be wondered that not more people have been put off, or that having once been put off, they ever come back.

But there have, of course, also been shortcomings on the part of those who have insisted on having nothing to do with the churches—such things, for example, as the cultural ignorance which has come from neglect of the

Scriptures, unexamined persistence in immature conceptions of God, excessive confidence in self, failure to support the churches and to strengthen the ministry (which you will remember was an original purpose for the founding of Harvard College), indifference, above all perhaps the loss of the practice of prayer.

It is no part of a college's obligation to endeavor to give or rather to impose answers, but a college should help her sons to ask the right questions—and all the questions. This is a very large and very difficult responsibility. For in my judgment this college or any college cannot properly discharge this responsibility if, because of a doctrinaire approach or a prejudiced view of the value of religion, it tends to concentrate attention on a part of human experience and abandons the effort to try to see it whole.

There was a time not so long ago when religious fundamentalism worked to prevent a free play of mind and spirit—was restrictive, unenlightened, fearful, limiting. Unfortunately there are those who honestly believe, in spite it seems to me of a vast amount of contrary evidence in music, art, and personal behavior, that religion's influence must always be of this nature. But with the advance of secularization there has come into being a new kind of fundamentalism, a secular variety. And whereas the old kind, at least in academic circles, has long since been unmasked and put to flight, the new kind, which would forcibly eschew all attention to religion, unfortunately has scarcely as yet been identified, with the result that its noxious influence—noxious I believe to spirit, imagination, and so also, in the long run, to mind—works among us almost unopposed, and at times indeed with approval.

We are members of a secular university in a society which, despite the many churches to be seen in all the

towns and cities in America, is fundamentally more secular than we like to admit. It does not follow from this
fact, however, that we should be afraid or scornful of
religion. It is as hard to explain human virtue in terms of
a secular world as it is to explain pain in terms of an
omnipotent God. And yet Harvard is still interested in
human virtue, even as in Dr. Peabody's day, and as eager
to see it grow in each of her sons. Mr. Oldham, coming
close to the very heart of the case for religion in a secular
society, speaks of "the infinite obligation men owe one
another."

The infinite obligation men owe one another? Why?
It seems to me that this must be for no other possible
reason than that God wills it so; for if it is not so from
Him, from the very center of the creativity in our world,
then it is not really so. In my judgment Mr. Oldham
illuminates the basic problem which is posed for us by the
advance of secularization in our time when he asks, "Why
should we rule out the possibility that the deepest secret
and meaning of life should be found, not in the exploration and manipulation of a world of things, but in com-
munication and dialogue, encounter and response?" To
this question it seems to me if we are truly thoughtful we
can only echo, "Why indeed?"

A college can only hope that in four years of untram-
melled study, in activity outside the classroom, in association with friends and perhaps in experience with church
membership, its influence has in some way helped the
student to find meaning and center for his life. If he has
found this outside religion, so long as he has found it for
himself, there can be no fault in that. Agnosticism can be
an honest and, at least in the face of false gods, an entirely
healthy state of mind. But the experience of many seems
to indicate that it is not a state of mind in which one can

long dwell, for trust we must in someone or something, surely for our spiritual and mental health; not merely in ourselves. The final answer must, we hope, be God.

Secularization, like cultural variety, has had the effect of making worship increasingly difficult for us. But it has not in my judgment made it irrelevant. Indeed it would seem to me to be a very superficial intellectual credo which would imply that the questions of religion can be ignored in or out of college. Let us hope that with all its generous offerings the college will not fail the student at this most crucial point, and that the total college experience of each undergraduate will help him again and again in years to come to realize the enlightenment and joy of belief.

* * * * * * *

UTILITY AND THE
AMERICAN UNIVERSITY

LESS THAN A CENTURY AGO we had no universities
in America—or at least none worthy of the name. The
oldest of the ones we now have were built in about four
decades following the Civil War. This was the period
when a variety of social changes produced some of the
major determinants of our lives today: the completion,
chiefly through immigration, of the settlement of the vast
continent across which our country now lies, the growth
of cities, the forging of our basic industrial economic
system, and our advance to world power. It is fair to say
that the development of our universities and these other
great national achievements were not unrelated.

One might ask, How did we come to have universities?
It is a complicated story, but we can see now that the
impetus for their creation came from a relatively small
number of informed and determined men—Tappan of
Michigan; Gilman, who headed California before he went
to Hopkins; Eliot of Harvard; White of Cornell; Barnard
of Columbia—and a few others.

These men were moved to their great undertaking by
contact with the superior intellectual achievement of universities abroad, chiefly the German universities of the
early nineteenth century. In the light of the first-hand

Address at the inauguration of Clark Kerr as President of the University
of California, held at the Los Angeles campus, September 26, 1958.

experiences they had with European university education, the colleges they had known in America came to seem to them little better than high schools. Here young, ill-prepared pedagogues conducted recitations based on uninspired textbooks, largely in the classics and mathematics, at very elementary levels. The European universities, in contrast, were communities of mature scholars who offered advanced lectures in their specialties. It came to Americans as a surprise to discover that in Europe the professors were admirable individuals occupying places of honor in society, who were not content simply to teach what was already known, but who took their chief delight in discovering fresh knowledge. It is from this excited discovery made by a few young American scholars abroad that our great university movement stems. There they met a new, and for them wonderful, world of mind, and straightway determined that we should have something like it here in America.

Starting where they could (with exception of the fresh designs at Johns Hopkins and Clark) they labored mightily to transform pre-existing colleges into universities. Their early attempts to widen the scope and deepen the content of the higher learning in America seem now to us to have a certain quaintness about them. For example, it is difficult to believe that a fierce, long-protracted struggle was required to win a place in the curriculum for modern languages alongside of the classics (though such has been our indifference to these studies latterly that a similar effort may soon have to be made again). We are also apt to laugh at stories of various early attempts to treat college students as adults rather than school children. But with the initiation of the change that was to transform the early college into something new the university's tempo soon accelerated and its reach extended.

The natural sciences were speedily successful in winning a larger place in the curriculum. Because of the prestige they gained through early dramatic achievements of some of those who cultivated them, scientific studies played a central role in bringing the American university to maturity. Their success also made it relatively easy later for the social sciences, as they became differentiated, to take up secure positions of independent strength within the curriculum. Applications of science followed at many points and came to be expected. Starting early and continuing through the whole period of development, largely because of pressures from the advancing social and economic life in America, a cluster of professional schools soon developed around the school of graduate studies. Thus despite the hostility and protests of its defenders— usually with very little support from any of those inside— the early American college here and there was slowly changed into a university, a new kind of institution among us, whose very life-blood was a combination of emphasis upon the central importance of investigation as contrasted with teaching coupled with a more specifically American notion that the work of the university should be related in an intimate way to pressing problems of society.

Such a brief account makes the development of the university in America out of the antecedent colonial college seem considerably more direct and simple than it was. Actually, while the process was going on, there was never anywhere in the country a single uniform idea of what a university should be. Nor was there any common practice in their building. It was widely recognized that universities had been made necessary by, and were supposed to serve, practical human needs, but there was very little agreement as to how this should be done. The difficulties President Gilman got into with the farmers of California may now seem a little ridiculous to us, but they certainly could not have seemed so to him. And a man like Ezra Cornell had endless obstacles in New York. For example, on one occasion he had to stand by and hear himself described in the legislature as a swindler who was trying to rob the public to build a monument to himself. At this point he is reported to have turned to Andrew Dickson White to whisper, "If I could think of any other way in which half a million of dollars would do as much good to the state"—the sums required to establish universities then were not so great!—"I would give the legislature no more trouble." Then he went on to say in a passage peculiarly poignant to me, "I am not sure but that it would be a good thing for me to give the half a million to old Harvard College in Massachusetts, to educate the descendants of the men who hanged my forefathers." Fortunately for Cornell, unfortunately for Harvard, Ezra was spared this act of final desperation. The contending parties found a modus vivendi, and the two men who were determined to give New York State a university got on with their task.

In one way or another our universities were built—as they are still being built. Today there is a whole network of them across the country. Staffed by scores of thousands of faculty members providing instruction for literally millions of undergraduates and many, many thousands of advanced students, the seats of an indescribable number of research efforts in every area of knowledge carried on both by individuals and by teams, the possessors of laboratories and libraries without which there is no way either to come into possession of knowledge or to hope to begin to undertake its advance, they stand among the chief assets of our country, scarcely less to be admired for their achievements to date than for the great promise still growing within them. As we come to them in our generation, we find entrusted to us institutions which have been wrought through the inspired and indomitable efforts of generations of devoted servants of the higher learning. At first these men were apt to be Christian missionaries and classical scholars such as California's Willey and Durant; then, more frequently, men set on fire by the new science; but always, early and late, a succession of individuals, in and out of public office with more than average foresight and concern, who were ready and eager to help wherever they could.

The work of building and advancing these institutions is still far from completed. Yet we now have serious reason to be concerned lest we think so intently of the need for buildings—for classrooms and dormitories—and for increased numbers of teachers to cope with the inevitable enormously enlarged numbers of students, that we shall forget that the indispensable first requirement for universities is not simply teachers, but *scholar* teachers. So it was in the beginning, so it is now. To be sure, we regularly pay lip service to this idea, but there is much in our practice to suggest that we are not really seriously impressed by the value—the worth and beauty—of disinterested inquiry. An endemic threat of indifference to the ideal is always present in America, and this is strengthened by a tendency widespread among us to think of the university as primarily a service institution, completely overlooking the fact that the institution's capacity to serve depends first upon its enjoyment of an independent life of its own.

It is easy to see how this situation came about. While the university was building in America, one of the arguments most frequently advanced in its support was the need for more adequate recognition by American higher education of the practical concerns of everyday life. This concern was perhaps never absent among us. Benjamin

Franklin introduced it in the eighteenth century and to a degree helped shape the character of the University of Pennsylvania. Thomas Jefferson in somewhat similar manner had at least momentary effect at the University of Virginia. George Ticknor propounded the argument at Harvard early in the nineteenth century, although without substantial influence on that conservative institution.

Thus the notion that a university should minister directly to the economic needs of society found its way early into the rationale underlying the contemporary American university. It was forwarded particularly by President Wayland of Brown and put into practice by White at Cornell and later by Van Hise at Wisconsin— for in a nation undergoing intense agricultural and industrial development the practical application of knowledge had an immediate appeal and made more understandable the need for advancing the still imperfectly understood and not immediately engaging idea of the university. There was of course merit in the case as presented. But, reiterated again and again, the argument soon came to be an unexamined article in the American credo touching the university, with the result that today it is not only accepted almost without question but at times seems to make the whole of the idea of an American university. And yet—as the founders of our universities would have been the first to insist—the university's true role is not, and cannot be, a servile one.

A university has to carry a great many young people through a variety of programs of undergraduate instruction—through programs of general education to help them grow as individuals and citizens, and of specialized education to help them forward in their professional interests. Of course—and this is an acceptable and exciting duty. This will also be a much larger obligation in the future than it has been in the past. A university has also to provide the many, many advanced kinds of professional education of which our society now stands so hungrily in need. Again we may say, of course. These responsibilities must be assumed without complaint. And there is place within the university's range of activity for a wide variety of institutes, clinics, and research activities of immediate practical significance. Everywhere in the world today there is a great hunger for the technical and material results of science, and from this has sprung up around the world an extraordinary new respect for, and a desire to have, universities. One sees this as clearly as anywhere in the great prominence given to the new university building in Moscow. Such enhanced respect is understandable, for the university has indeed demonstrated an extraordinary aptitude for ministering to material human needs, as well as to problems of defense, and this seems to be at the moment what is chiefly wanted from it. But this was not what first called it into existence, nor can it in my judgment ever safely be thought to provide the sum or substance of its aim.

A university was, and is, first of all an association of scholars. It is their essential function not to produce goods or perform practical services, but simply to keep a life of mind vigorous and functioning among us. Though it is a cardinal article in this basic faith that from this kind of activity, pre-eminently, other kinds of goods now associated with the university are apt to flow, the first justification for it is not this, but simply that mental activity of this sort becomes our full humanity. And it behooves us now, beset by practical concerns, to remember that this kind of activity especially, justified in its own right, enlivens and deepens the university and draws forth the new adventures and achievements of mind which sustain its life.

At such a time as the present, when the outward and visible concerns of the university make such extraordinary and insistent demands on our attention, we need especially to recall that the true worth of a university is finally to be measured not by the number of its campuses, the variety of its programs, the number of its students, or its ability to be of service to outside interests, but by the number and quality of its advanced scholars and by the vigor, imaginative boldness, and precision of their individual intellectual endeavors. What is really of consequence is their capacity as a community to take thought for the whole of what man has learned, to keep it known and extend it, to stimulate each other, and—here we come upon a very special educational function of the university—to train their own, a growing number of successors who will be no less committed to scholarship or less quick of intellect than themselves.

This was true at the university's beginning in America. It is no less true today. Indeed, because of the vastly increased complexity both of knowledge and of society, because also of our more precarious and responsible position in the world, and finally because of the rapidly increasing need among us for scholarship of the highest order in every field at its most advanced and difficult levels, we shall do well to begin now to insist less on what was in part always an argument *ad hominem* and—in mature recognition of the unconditioned value of learning—talk less about what the university can do for the state and ask rather more frequently, seriously, and consistently, what can our states do to strengthen their universities for their essential tasks?

Those who worked to establish the university among us were moved to the task by their admiration for the professors of high scholarly attainment whom they met abroad and with whom the teachers they had known at home in American colleges were not to be compared. It was their view that to bring together groups of such scholars, men of talent and wide learning who found their life work and their chief pleasure in scholarship, was to create a university. To be sure, they had no idea of the number of scholars which would presently be required as the fields of the known and the about-to-be-known divided, multiplied, and grew; nor of what a costly business it would soon become to provide the libraries, laboratories —yes, and also the graduate students—they would need. But they had no uncertainty about the main point, that basically it was the association of mature scholars which was the university; nor about the fact that they would do their best work only in an atmosphere of freedom.

Today our universities are beset by all kinds of practical concerns. The professions want their graduates. Industry and government expect scholarly attention devoted to their needs. This seems unavoidable and steadily grows more intense. There is indubitably some life-giving quality in these circumstances. There can be too-great fastidiousness in the intellectual activity of a university, and warmth, sanity, and vigor can come into scholarship from close contact with the activities and aspirations of daily life. There is no reason to deny that the initial impetus toward many of the research efforts now going forward at any moment in a university can come safely from outside —from the needs of the military, or industry, or from some other quarter of our complex society; but never in my judgment should all or even a preponderant part of our research programs so derive. For the kind of research effort which alone can safely maintain the life of a true university is the one into which an imaginative scholar is led not by outside pressures but by his own curiosity.

We who enjoy the fruits of scientific discovery occasionally marvel at the grand vision, the flash of insight which enables a man like Charles Babbage to conceive of both the "difference engine" and the "analytical engine" and then spend a disappointing lifetime trying to make the concepts work. Yet from Babbage's labors and from the host of influences which helped shape his life, including his formal education at Cambridge University, can be said to spring the research which has brought us to an age of computers of whose electronic power Babbage could only dream, and whose potentialities were left to be developed by others—men such as Aiken at Harvard and von Neuman at Princeton.

Similarly we have built a whole new world of physics and chemistry since the discovery of the X ray and the atomic nucleus near the turn of the century. The building blocks bear names such as Becquerel, Rutherford, the Curies, Cockcroft and Walton, Hahn and Strassmann, and many others. But no man in this country had more initial influence than the late E. O. Lawrence of California, who, with Livingston, found the means of accelerating charged particles to high energies and made it possible to transmute heavier elements through the use of cyclotron bombardment. This touched off a whole host of new studies which in turn led to the discovery of how to make plutonium and the beginning of the nuclear age.

The revolutionary relationship of learning to life is never limited exclusively to science. A whole range of new explorations into the mind and culture of a nation can emerge from the gradual building of an historical tradition at a university. We have witnessed this at Har-

vard, progressing through the work of men like Jared
Sparks, Henry Adams, Edward Channing, Frederick Jackson Turner, Albert Bushnell Hart, Samuel Eliot Morison,
the senior Schlesinger, and Frederick Merk down to the
present generation and broadening into scholarly examination of the whole of American history, literature, and
life!

Similarly in medicine, the juxtaposition of a professional school with the working world of the hospital can,
out of hundreds and hundreds of individual disinterested
researches and the busy lives of men like Minot, Cannon,
Cushing, and Zinsser, create a new direction and fresh
spirit of human service in the world. And these accom-
plishments which I know from Harvard can be matched
elsewhere.

Surely the greatest intellectual achievements and discoveries of man come from the cumulative effect of isolated efforts by different individuals working on special
problems which puzzle and intrigue them. And their long-
range influence is always great because of the spark of
intellectual power which was mysteriously transmitted
to their associates and their students, or to those who study
the record of their work.

Our chief present need is not simply for "teachers"—
for individuals whose function it is to man classrooms to
help young people through grades, over the various academic hurdles decreed by custom, and so into lucrative
professional activity. This would be to revert to that
totally unacceptable, indeed ignorant, understanding of
the higher learning which drove the founders of our universities to revolt. But it is for scholar-teachers whose joy
shall be in the free play of mind, and who alone, because
of their zeal for learning and devotion to it, can be adequate for the extraordinarily complicated intellectual de-

mands of our time. What we need above all is an awareness in society which will lead to a multiplication of *their* kind. America's universities—begun so late, developed with enormous difficulty in the face of inadequate understanding, now grown to magnificent estate—are to be numbered among her greatest resources, more powerful in the ideas which can come from them than factories, dams, or reservoirs of oil. For their proper functioning they need within them people of imagination and daring who will find their greatest happiness in carrying on their own intellectual quests. But they also need people outside— many of them—who will understand and happily accept the fact that learning is apt to be most useful, even within professional schools, when it does not aim too intently or too directly at the goal of immediate utility.

To my mind the truly urgent need confronting higher education in America today is first for wide recognition that the university requires for its proper functioning an independent life of its own; that is, for a generous understanding of the fact that a university's basic intellectual activity cannot be an accessory activity serving other interests than those of the free play of mind; and then for a willing acceptance of the consequences in action which must follow from this recognition.

Time will tell if this is a utopian hope. It is still to be demonstrated that a great democratic nation can come to a sustained realization of the need to nurture and perpetuate creative intellectual activity, to an appreciation of its value, and to an honest experience of its enjoyment freed from pressing and constricting utilitarian concern.

* * * * * * *

THE JOINT RESPONSIBILITY OF
PUBLIC AND PRIVATE
UNIVERSITIES

O NE IS FOREVER encountering an assumption that public and private institutions are somehow, or should be, engaged in deadly combat. Partisans on the one side, for example, are not above trying to establish the idea that state universities are godless, socialistic institutions for promoting statism; or, on the other, that private universities are undemocratic citadels of aristocratic privilege. Such statements seem to me to be invidious nonsense. Nor do I find more acceptable claims that state institutions are the only ones concerned to provide educational opportunities for the poor and ambitious, or that private institutions are alone suited to furnish the kind of education required for the exceptionally able.

State universities are older than is commonly thought. Twenty-one of them were founded before the Civil War, beginning with Georgia in 1785 and North Carolina in 1789. Thus, if length of residence among us is an indication of American character, surely these institutions are as "American" as any. When one recalls that there were only nine institutions of higher learning established in colonial America, it is also clear that a number of the

Address at the inauguration of Charles Edwin Odegaard as President of the University of Washington, November 7, 1958.

public institutions have as much claim to the dignity and respect of age as do most of the private ones.

At the outset all of the state universities had to struggle against indifference—and frequently, too, against active hostility—to get themselves established. They had to keep on struggling to survive. The beginnings of none of them, no more than the beginnings of most of the private ones, were especially impressive. For example we are told that in its early years the University of North Carolina had a twenty-four-year-old president and a faculty of three, consisting of "a French ex-monk, a deserter from the British navy, and a strolling player." It would be interesting to know what subjects each of them taught.

But in time the state universities came of age. There are several markers to indicate steps along the way. One was the opening of the University of Virginia in 1825. Another was the work of Henry P. Tappan at Michigan in the 1850's. A third was the passage of the Morrill Act in 1862 which enabled several of the state universities, by keeping the land grants in their own hands, for the first time substantially to strengthen themselves. Perhaps for most the time of majority was to come still later. In any event, nowhere before the Civil War did state legislatures provide serious or steady support for their universities.

Today there are many state universities, the majority of them strong and large. Together they carry a considerable part of the total burden of higher education in America. I suspect even the most partisan supporter of private institutions, if he has actually looked at the other kind recently, will have to agree that in all likelihood they are here to stay.

A point apparently imperfectly understood about state universities is that they were not imposed upon our country by a special interest group, but rather grew in response to valid educational needs. Though it is of course obvious that these institutions were intended to provide more educational opportunity, it is an oversimplification to say that their primary purpose was to make it possible for poor boys to go to college. Indeed, the many small, privately supported, denominational colleges which predated the state universities were perhaps better designed, because of their low costs and wide dispersion, to fill this role. As a matter of fact it was not uncommon in the early years of the state universities to find the partisans of the private colleges hurling the nasty epithet "aristocratic" at state universities, because they did not in the beginning offer free tuition and often were more attractive to the sons of the wealthy than were the small colleges. It is impossible not to conclude that from the beginning both kinds of institutions could and did under varying circumstances offer educational opportunity to both pecunious and impecunious students, just as they do today.

There were other deeper reasons which stimulated the birth of state universities. One was the justified complaint that the curriculum of the small denominational college was narrow and excessively "literary" because it was rooted solely in Greek, Latin, and mathematics—in keeping with an academic tradition designed centuries before to meet the needs of young men most of whom were preparing for the ministry or for teaching. It is not fair completely to condemn this course of study because, like programs of liberal education in any age, it simply eschewed vocational concern to concentrate on helping individuals, by cultivating their minds and widening their interests, to live wisely, happily, and well. This early curriculum had, and has, its merits. But as the country grew, and economic interests and professions multiplied, it became increasingly difficult to maintain that it was and should always be the only curriculum. And since there was almost no disposition within the early college to alter or widen the accepted body of courses, a movement for a new kind of institution, less bound by tradition, understandably got under way.

The small denominational college was also thought to be inadequate because of its religious particularity. Founded by and intended to serve the interests of special groups, these institutions all too frequently permitted questions of church membership to weigh too heavily in what were primarily educational concerns, and they never succeeded in throwing off the suspicion of partiality. Again it is not surprising that many felt a need for a new kind of higher learning which would belong, as it was said, to "all the people" above, or outside, sectarian control. Incidentally, this should not be understood to imply, as their self-regarding opponents were even then not above asserting, that the desired publicly supported institutions set out deliberately to be "godless."

Still another shortcoming of the older privately supported institutions of higher learning which helped forward the movement for state universities was faculty resistance to change. Fierce and suspicious faculty opposition often greeted the ambitious efforts of enlightened presidents and teachers to turn these colleges into universities—to make them communities not of pedagogues giving elementary instruction but of mature scholars. In a very real sense the movement for state universities was thus only part of a larger movement in the United States to establish here institutions of truly higher learning, built after continental models, which because of their advanced scholarship would really deserve the name of "university." Incidentally, we are again in a period in which this proud name is being bestowed rather lightly, at times it would seem almost barbarically. But however that may be, much of the leadership in this effort which produced true universities among us for the first time came from private institutions. The strongest of them, together with new private institutions such as Hopkins and later Chicago, succeeded as well as any in growing to meet the new standard. Indeed they led the way. But they were flanked by a number of public institutions, originally little better than colleges, which, beginning in the seventies and eighties of the last century, succeeded in transforming themselves into true universities.

Thus the state university movement, appealing to a wider range of interest and concern and calling for a wider curriculum, for increased emphasis on science, and for more and more research, was a movement for a new kind of institution in our land whose distinction would be as much in the quality of its advanced scholarship as in the reach of its quantitative appeal.

Still a further and utterly practical reason why many individuals thought the private institutions could not by themselves furnish the higher education our nation required was their weak financial backing. Up to the Civil War some 516 colleges had been established in the sixteen states of the Union but of this number only 104 have survived. One has only to look back a short time to Principal Mercer's frontier "university" in the days before Washington's statehood to grasp how great was the difference between the vision and the realization in the founding era of state universities. As a contemporary observer said, "[Colleges] are duly lauded and puffed for a day; and then they sink to be heard of no more."

Early advocates of state-supported institutions were appalled by the proliferation of small sectarian colleges and shocked by the constricted financial limitations within which virtually all of them had to struggle. The achievement of strong education, it seemed to them, called for concentration of resources, and they were fully persuaded that higher education was of such importance to the people that a state must adequately support it. Only after these institutions won consistent financial support—as Michigan and Wisconsin among early examples—did they grow strong in state after state, and contribute to the impressive, if perhaps still inadequate, network of substantial institutions we have today.

It seems almost superfluous to say that ample and consistent financing is essential for all educational institutions with convictions of excellence. There have been some private institutions which have demonstrated ability to get such support without benefit of tax income, or with only very meager help from this source; but it has also been clearly demonstrated that an adequate share of tax income is a powerful encouragement to the development of strong publicly supported institutions of higher learning. It is to be hoped, therefore, that both kinds of support, now inextricably mixed, will continue and increase, and that the two kinds of institutions, both provided with ample resources, will continue to advance.

Thus far my argument has led me to concentrate attention on their similarities, but there are also significant points of difference between public and private institutions. Among these are differences in tradition, in the percentage of their income derived from different sources, in the range of their responsibilities, in their educational emphases, in the kinds of pressures that play upon them, above all in their forms of control. And these are important. We in the private institutions believe strongly that it is essential for the health of the whole of higher education in America that there always be strong private colleges and universities kept safely beyond the reach of political control. We recognize that the best of the relatively small private colleges are as successful as any institutions in the pursuit of excellence. We do not agree, however, that only small colleges are concerned for their students as individuals. But we feel it is especially important for the health of our total educational enterprise that large private universities which have acquired extraordinary educational resources, and which have served the highest educational standards over a long period of time, continue strong and independent. By concentrating their attention, or perhaps it is fair to say, by neglecting obligations which a state university cannot neglect, they have a special capacity sometimes to move more quickly in pursuit of new interests and can work more consistently and more single-mindedly to advance standards. These capacities are important for the whole of higher education. But we know, too, that in the past private institutions have many times been helped to awareness of new responsibility and pushed from narrowness, complacency, and conservatism by the competition of state universities; and we suspect (and hope) this may also be true again and again. Nor should anything I have said here be understood to imply that the highest standards of academic performance cannot also be served, even at the most creative levels, in public institutions.

Some years ago a Harvard report on general education spoke of Jeffersonian and Jacksonian emphases within our educational practice, "the one valuing opportunity as the nurse of excellence, the other as the guard of equity." It is easy to assert that at the level of higher education one of these functions belongs to one kind of institution, the other to the other, but to do so is to ignore the facts. There are strong public institutions pursuing the highest standards of academic excellence along with strong private

ones, and there are many in both groups which fall below
—some far below—such standards. One can say the same
thing about large or small institutions of higher learning.
Some small ones are strong and some are weak, some large
ones are weak and some are strong. Neither pretensions
nor stereotypes fit the facts. After centuries of development, about all we can say is that there are a great many
sorts of differences within differing types of educational
institutions. It is perhaps time, therefore, that we abandon
unwarranted, broad generalizations and learn instead to
look at each institution for what it is in itself.

We have been told again and again that we shall need
in a relatively short time to provide for at least twice as
many students as we have acquired the capacity to care
for during more than three hundred years of effort. This
is true. We shall also need the added resources to make
this possible. And we shall have to meet tightening demands for an enormous range of technical and professional training, and while doing so, and seeking to meet
the other legitimate utilitarian expectations confronting
our universities at every turn, we shall have to fight to
strengthen liberal learning and to extend its influence in
every part of our endeavor. We must also, in the national
interest, carry more exceptionally talented, ambitious, and
dedicated individuals to higher peaks of learning and intellectual interest in many more areas of knowledge than
our fathers or grandfathers ever dreamed of. Indeed in
view of our present situation in the world it would be
almost treasonable now to say simply that we need more
educational opportunity for more individuals in terms of
what we might call "ordinary" post-high school education;
for at the same time we also need more opportunity for
able and willing students to go forward to the most difficult, most advanced, most demanding, and most creative

kinds of learning—to levels which require extraordinary ability, prolonged concentration of effort, and indomitable ambition. To dismiss or neglect this part of our responsibility with the smear word that its pursuance somehow implies the formation of an "élite" seems to me vicious demagoguery. At the same time, the contrary notion that institutions which profess to be devoted to the pursuit of quality have no share in the quantitative aspect of our problem seems to me equally misguided and unrealistic.

It was fortunate for the nation that, in the period between the Civil War and World War I, when our country as we know it today was coming of age, there were numerous leaders in higher education who, despite occasional differences and varying approaches, labored to adapt to American conditions and traditions the vision of the European university, with its emphases upon quality of research and teaching and upon excellence of professional training. Some of the great universities which resulted were private, others public. The roster of names of the builders of these institutions includes men like Tappan of Michigan, White of Cornell, Folwell of Minnesota, Gilman of California and Johns Hopkins, Van Hise of Wisconsin, Angell of Yale, Harper of Chicago, and Eliot of Harvard. They were the heroes and champions of a truly higher, higher education for America, and it is to them above all that we owe thanks that we now have a widespread public-private university system adequate, we hope, to cope with the enormously more complicated problems of our age.

Our public and our private institutions, created through a variety of circumstances over a long period of time, are now inescapably involved in joint responsibility. If they are competing, it is the friendly competition of two workers on one project. Inseparable considerations of quality and quantity touch education at every point; both make valid claims on every institution. It is therefore necessary for each institution within both groups to do what it can, honestly and intelligently, to make a contribution to the solution of both aspects of our problem. Surely in view of its immensity and urgency we can do better now than to waste time in misrepresentation, or in injurious, disputatious hostility among ourselves.

There are a number of things we can do together. We can cooperate within states and in the nation to help governments establish sound educational policies. We can work to prevent duplication of effort in research, in teaching, and in the preservation of books, documents, and other collections which are the tools of teaching and research. We can work together to extend opportunity, to open education to more and more who are qualified, and higher and higher education to the highly able who can be encouraged to pursue it. Above all we can work together to create better general understanding of the nature and need for higher education, and to obtain more generous support for it.

To me our most pressing present problem is to promote this kind of understanding. At the very beginning of the movement to establish state universities, forces within the world of higher education working against qualitative achievement were given new strength. The movement to widen educational opportunity brought with it, in Professor Hofstadter's words, a certain "disdain for authority and excellence and *expertise* of all kinds." Mr. Hofstadter appropriately quotes President Francis Wayland of Brown, who said at the very outset of the university movement in America that "the old practice of assigning academic rank at commencement had often been 'dropped like a polluted thing' because administrators were 'awed by the hoarse growl of popular discontent.' " As early as 1855 the President of the University of Georgia remarked that the American people were "generally satisfied with the *name* of a college, and sought for their sons not so much an education as a degree."

There is indeed much for all in higher education to do if at this moment of our history we are to give America's young people not the name but the experience of higher education, and give the nation the kinds of educated individuals she now so seriously needs. Among our public and private universities there are some with a particularly deep concern and a larger share of responsibility for the upper reaches and more demanding kinds of higher education. It is my sincere hope that we in the private institutions can stand shoulder to shoulder with the publicly supported institutions and together face hopefully and determinedly the grave responsibility before us both.

* * * * * * *

SCIENCE IN THE UNIVERSITY

ONE OF THE MOST DRAMATIC CHANGES in the activity of universities during the past two decades has been in the amount of their effort and of their resources now devoted to research, especially to research in the sciences. Thirty years ago, when the total education and general expenses of all the institutions of higher learning in the United States were $378 million, these institutions were spending only $18 million, or about 5 per cent of their total educational and general expenses, on organized research. Today, when their total expenditures in these categories have risen to nearly $3 billion, they are spending almost 20 per cent of greatly enlarged budgets, or more than a half *billion* dollars, for this purpose. Another way of saying this is that during this short period the universities' effort in research has increased more than thirty-two times.

The increase in attention devoted to research by industry and government is even more marked. Thirty years ago as a nation we were spending $170 million, or two-tenths of one per cent of a gross national product of $91 billion, on research and development. In 1957 we spent two and three-tenths per cent of a gross national product of 434 billions, or ten billion dollars, for these purposes. Only a small part of this—less than half a billion dollars of it—was expended in colleges and universities, great as

Address at a dinner meeting of the Economic Club of New York in the Waldorf Astoria Hotel, April 21, 1959.

is the increase in the amount of their effort now devoted to research.

It is perhaps worth noting in passing that four cents out of every dollar in the entire federal budget now goes for research and development. This is double the proportion spent ten years ago. The sum involved annually is now in the neighborhood of $3 billion. More than 60 per cent of this goes for development; less than 40 per cent for research; but hardly 4 per cent for what one might honestly call basic research, as this term is understood in universities. I am prepared to believe that in the circumstances in which our lives are cast at present this pattern of allocation is perhaps inevitable. But these circumstances do not free us from the necessity to try to understand what we are and are not spending our money on.

Many of you, I suppose, were, like me, brought up in awe of the discoveries of men like Robert Koch and Louis Pasteur, who showed the relationship of microbes to disease and to natural processes like fermentation. In their work the fact that microbes had to be nurtured in a "culture" of meat extract was purely incidental to the scientific study of the control and use of bacteria for the benefit of mankind.

But as far back as 1922, a year before he came to Harvard, a young man named J. Howard Mueller began to speculate as to the connection between the growth of bacteria in the meat broth and the nutrients in the broth. If the growth of micro-organisms was affected by the constituents in the broth, were there not biochemical compounds to be studied here which significantly influence living things? Since these substances originally came from animal tissue, what role did they play there?

The first fruit of this approach, coming very quickly, was the discovery of methionine, a previously unknown compound which is essential in the diet of man as well as of many bacteria. And here one sees how quickly and easily pure research and applied science come together; for the low content of methionine in vegetable proteins is an important factor contributing to the poor nutritional state of millions of people in the more crowded parts of the world; and the modern chemical industry is now engaged in efforts to synthesize methionine cheaply enough to permit its use as a dietary supplement on a large scale.

We can carry Mueller's work one step further. He proved the value of using micro-organisms to spy out the secrets of the higher animal, on the assumption that organisms at the two extremes of the evolutionary spectrum would utilize at least some identical compounds in their economy. During subsequent decades, research has continued to demonstrate the far-reaching unity of biology at the biochemical level.

In all living forms, proteins and other giant molecules responsible for characteristic differences among various organisms are shown to be made of the same building blocks, whether they be in bacteria, plants, or human brain cells. What is more, it has also been found that the major biochemical processes by which these compounds are made, and the sources of the energy required for these processes, are also largely identical throughout the biological kingdom.

Even more exciting results have come from using micro-organisms in the study of genetics, where it has also been shown that the fundamental mechanisms responsible for inheritance are the same in micro-organisms and in higher organisms. It has proved possible with bacteria to purify the chemical substance responsible for heredity and then to introduce it into cells and observe its effect on their hereditary properties. The discovery of the genetic role of

this remarkable acid called DNA was made in 1942 by
Avery at the Rockefeller Institute. The importance of
Avery's discovery was soon recognized by nonmedical
biologists. Since then the work of Dr. James Watson of
Harvard and of many others has contributed to an understanding of the mechanism by which DNA can duplicate
itself faithfully in every cell division. These studies, more
than any other approach, have reached close to the heart
of the problem of the nature of living material.

There is more to be said about the victories for knowledge which have been won by microbiologists and the increased promise which now lies in continuing studies of
micro-organisms, particularly at the moment, for the better understanding of cell physiology; but I turn now to a
different field to suggest the way in which the research
chain can run from discovery to development and then
again from development to discovery, in and out of universities. Undoubtedly the most famous example of this
in our time would be that of nuclear fission which
stemmed from Einstein's theory of relativity and had to
be discovered and understood before an atomic bomb or
other products of nuclear reaction could be developed.
However, I should like to mention something closer to
home.

During World War II Harvard and the Massachusetts
Institute of Technology were intimately associated in the
development of the radar principle. M.I.T.'s radiation
laboratory was busy producing new radar instrumentation
as fast as possible, and Harvard's counter measures laboratory was just as busy devising ways to make the new equipment useless—also as fast as possible—on the assumption,
of course, that the enemy might be before us with the
offensive tools.

At that time Harvard's Nobel laureate, Edward Purcell,

was working in the M.I.T. Radiation Laboratory. He and others had a part in developing microwave radar which made possible a new approach to the study of molecular structure. After the war, a dozen or so men were engaged in microwave examination of molecules, but soon the feasible range of extension of this study became distinctly limited. It then fell to Professor Bright Wilson and his associates in the Harvard Chemistry Department to devise a machine known as the stark effect microwave spectrograph which all at once gave almost unlimited range to the structural analysis of molecules and maintained the intense interest of scientists in this field.

One of these researchers who used the Wilson instrument was Charles Townes of Columbia [now Provost of the Massachusetts Institute of Technology], who, with Gordon, constructed the ammonia gas maser. This device, depending in part on the work with molecular beams done by Rabi of Columbia and Ramsey of Harvard, was intended to amplify microwaves by stimulated emission of radiation. The ammonia maser proved a practical means of calibrating atomic clocks, but because of "low power" was not adapted to the engineering requirements for amplification, since great intensities of amplification are possible only in the solid rather than the gaseous state. In the summer of 1956, however, Nicholas Bloembergen of Harvard, whose work stemmed in some measure from the research of Van Vleck of Harvard on the fundamental theory of paramagnetism, suggested the fundamental basis on which a solid-state maser could be constructed. This idea was adopted by the Bell Telephone Laboratories, which used its personnel and funds to produce the first actual working solid-state maser.

Thus from the first studies of microwaves, in a series of steps and variant approaches, came a device which already promises to have revolutionary potentialities in radio astronomy, microwave propagation of telephone messages, early-warning ground radar, tracking of satellites, and so on. This practical device was made possible in the first instance not by organized research with purpose in mind but simply because college professors were interested in using radar as a tool to study the properties of matter. It was the culmination of twenty years of theoretical and experimental work at Harvard involving physics, chemistry, and engineering—a result of a curious interplay of developmental need and basic research, but essentially a fruit of disinterested professorial inquiry.

Perhaps these few examples of the pursuit of science in a university provide sufficient background for the few conclusions I should like now to attempt.

It is admittedly very difficult, if not impossible, to separate science from the applications of science. The first computing machines were put together by scholars who simply wanted to know. The iron lung was developed by a professor in a university school of public health, an institution which by definition is a curious compound of disinterested scientific inquiry and intense practical concern. There are many such examples; but development and science are not the same thing, nor science and technology, nor science and engineering, even though these things are apt to be lumped together by popular misunderstanding into an undifferentiated whole. The university's primary concern is not for the results of engineering, nor for science as an instrument of technology, but rather, essentially, for science as an intellectual pursuit whose compelling motive is simply the desire to know.

Universities have not always been congenial homes for the nurture of science. They had very little to do with initiating the great scientific revolution of modern times;

even less with the technological revolution which built
the world in which we live and from which we now expect
so much. They were late in turning to science, but they
have for at least a century been deeply concerned for it.
The result is that today in the United States they provide
the best homes and, although there are a few exceptions
like the Rockefeller Institute for Medical Research and
the Bell Laboratories, the universities are almost the only
places where basic science is a matter of unremitting,
primary concern.

The other day a Boston newspaper carried a story
headed "Chemists test 40,000 compounds yearly to find
cure for cancer." Here is a clear indication of what science
in a university is not. Its aim is not to find something
which will work in solving a practical problem. Certainly
it is not properly engaged in routine investigations routinely carried out. Its aim is rather to seek everlastingly for
fundamental explanations, to keep working at basic levels
until men are able to understand fully and deeply the
processes of nature. And it is this kind of inquiry, not
immediately concerned with applications, for which in
the long run we have essential need.

Truly basic science requires a special kind of scientist
and a congenial environment for his work. One of the most
frustrating characteristics of basic science, for the man
impatient for the results of science, is that it cannot be
planned. But such is the case. One of our most distinguished scientists recently went so far as to say that
"planned research is nonsense." Outside the university in
America the scientist is usually pursuing some end dic-
tated by his sponsor. There is of course pressing need for
countless such workers in our almost incomprehensible
multitude and variety of scientific activities. But for these
men the ends may quickly and suddenly change. It is al-

most solely in the university that the basic scientist is free
initially to work on problems of his choosing and free also
to turn at any moment from what he has been doing to
pursue a new path, whenever he feels so inclined, if the
new way looks promising to him. If he were inhibited by
having a purpose in his research other than that of simply
adding to knowledge, he would not turn aside, and the
chance for a new beginning would be lost. As we have all
come to know, the great triumphs of science develop
slowly from very small beginnings. The university's interest in science is to foster pregnant small beginnings. In the
great scientific effort of our country the work of university
science proceeds on a time scale which reaches beyond the
moment. It is perhaps for this reason that, though small
in scope, it is of crucial importance.

There are one or two more things which must be said.
Probably nine out of every ten major books of chemistry,
physics, or biology, at every level, come from universities.
Thus despite the tremendous growth of American industrial research it is the university which also plays the
major role in generalizing, synthesizing and disseminating
scientific knowledge. And beyond this is an even more
important consideration. It is the university—the university and the colleges which feed it—which together nurture and train the scientists and research workers for
tomorrow. For this indispensable process, involvement in
the kind of basic research which is carried on in universities by their best scientists is an almost essential pre-
requisite.

It is also a happy corollary that not infrequently our
best research scientists themselves thrive on the stimula-
tion provided them by first-rate, inquiring student minds.
In the favoring climate of universities the minds of young
people can be completely on science and find free play for

the imaginative ideas which so often lead to systematic organized scientific development outside universities. The interplay of idealistic enthusiasm and keen imagination between young students and their elders provokes the fructifying experience of discovery. It is not least for this reason that the truly devoted university scientist prefers his laboratory and his classroom to the often greater material rewards found outside the university. There is no question in his mind that the university atmosphere is better suited to the advanced training of scientists than what he supposes is a more limiting opportunity outside the university.

There is finally the question of support for science in the university. The free search for knowledge costs money. We have, to begin with, some funds of our own. These have increasingly in recent years been supplemented by helpful assistance from industry. But there can be no doubt that we are now coming into a period where the major source of support for science both inside and outside the universities will have to be the federal government. This does not mean expecting government aid at every turn, but it does mean that in particularly expensive areas like medicine and nuclear research the government in its own self-interest will wish to bear a major share of the cost.

There have been few institutions so wary of governmental invasion of the free search for knowledge as Harvard. Yet Harvard science—basic science—would not be where it is today had it not been for the aid of the Office of Naval Research, the National Science Foundation, the National Institutes of Health, and the Atomic Energy Commission, among others. Our new biochemical laboratories are being built largely by government help. For the first time, next year more than half of the activity of our

School of Public Health will be government-sponsored. And M.I.T. and Harvard will share joint responsibility for operation of the giant Cambridge Electron Accelerator sponsored by the AEC and located just north of the Harvard Yard. The instruments of modern science—the computers, the cyclotrons, and the accelerators—and the buildings to house them are beyond the capacities of even our wealthiest universities.

But there are good ways for government departments to spend money in universities for the advance of science, and there are bad ways. A number of Harvard scientists are particularly grateful to one government department, the Office of Naval Research. This agency has been supporting scientific activity in universities for as long as any, and from our point of view its efforts have been among the best. It certainly understands professors and above all is willing to make commitments over an extended period of time and forego impatient demands for "results." As a part of its activity it has wisely chosen to back productive scholars of proven capacity in lines of their special interest and competence. It is this kind of backing, based on full appreciation of scientists and the way basic science proceeds, which is most welcome to us and, we believe, in the long run will be most helpful to the nation. Backing of this kind gives the scientist confidence and frees him from the burdensome and wasteful necessity of making yearly special plans, special budgets, and special appeals for funds. The chief complaint heard in university circles about much government support of research is concerning its radical fluctuations rather than its restricted purpose. Long-term commitments are imperative, if promising and fruitful research is to be nourished—though it cannot be said that the government does not understand this. The trouble comes from the fact that government expenditures are tied to annual budget requirements, with the result that the wisest intentions are frustrated. And all too often the basic research programs—least obviously "practical"—are the first to feel the axe of economy. There is needed a way out of this impasse.

Our country is involved in a more serious life-and-death struggle than any of those who have been before us could have imagined. The frustrating and discouraging aspect of the contest is that there is no way we can get hold of its difficulties to uproot and exorcise them once for all. Instead, they appear to be with us for a long time to come.

It is the responsibility of the United States Department of Defense to provide for our immediate safety. In this realm our dependence is clearly on technology and the implements which technology can supply. In this endeavor the universities are also inextricably involved. But beyond the contesting forces of men and nations there is the quiet, nobler rivalry of the enterprise of science, evoking at a higher plane those moments of truth and knowledge on which the human race has ever built its loftiest aspirations. In this contest in the realm of mind, the goals are only good and the combatants conscious solely of discovery for discovery's sake. This is as it must be if science is to grow and continue to unfold the wonder of man and his surrounding universe. Science of this truly basic kind —unconcerned for the imperative demands of the moment—is of enormous long-range importance to us and to the world, both for defense and for fulfillment. It is my hope that we, as a people, shall continue to be able to find the wisdom, and the patience, needed for this kind of science's proper nurture and support.

* * * * * * *

COLLEGE EDUCATION AND
MORAL CHARACTER

HARVARD'S EARLY PRESIDENTS were all active members of the teaching faculty. The first president, President Dunster, who assumed the office in 1640, was for several years himself virtually the entire faculty, though he came in time to have the assistance of a few tutors, young men perhaps not quite so old nor perhaps quite so experienced as today's teaching fellows. Before the early nineteenth century there were very few professors—mature scholars—appointed at Harvard, or anywhere in this country, to help the president and tutors. Today's large faculties of senior scholars are of comparatively recent origin.

The early president was not only teacher, he was also preacher. He was invariably a minister, for religion was central in the life of the early college, and the president was taxed with the chief responsibility for the spiritual well-being of the whole community, of faculty as well as students. Nor did his involvement end there, for in addition discipline, administration, housekeeping—all the manifold problems so neatly subdivided for contemporary college leaders—fell to his lot.

As time went on, and as the colleges grew both in size and in resources, more and more individuals came to

Baccalaureate Sermon for the senior class of Harvard College, Harvard Memorial Church, June 7, 1959.

share the teaching burden. The president tended then to confine his teaching responsibility to the work of the senior year. In some of the smaller colleges for a long time the whole of the student's instruction in his last year continued to be entrusted to the president; in all of them, almost without exception, the major effort for every student in the senior year was a course in moral philosophy invariably taught by the president. In almost every college this course marked the climax of the undergraduate curriculum.

There was very little uncertainty in the mind of anyone connected with the early college in America about the purpose of its effort. The aim, universally acknowledged, was to advance religion. But two more immediate aims were also recognized as paths which had to be traversed as one moved toward the ultimate goal. One of these was to train the mind; the other, to develop moral character.

The educational theory (we would say the "models") which supported the practice of the early college saw the mind at one time as an instrument to be sharpened, at another as a storehouse to be filled. This theory explains, from the one view, the early college's endless practice of recitation, and from the other, its emphasis on the memorization of classical texts.

President Jeremiah Day of Yale concisely stated the first aim of the college in his Report of the Yale Faculty in 1828: "A commanding object in a collegiate course," he said, "should be to call into daily and vigorous exercise the faculties of the student." There were no lectures in the early college during which the student could relax in secure silence to think his own thoughts when his attention wandered.

Along with exercise of the faculties went filling the mind, for almost everyone then believed there was a fixed,

limited, and identifiable body of knowledge the acquisition of which marked the educated man. Some of today's
efforts toward more integrated curricula would seem to
owe something to nostalgia for this earlier, simpler state
of affairs.

But the mind was only part of the early educator's responsibility. Of greater concern was moral character. It is
difficult for us to conceive how prominently this phase
figured in discussions of education in those days. We tend
almost instinctively to shy away from the subject, or at
least to pass it by in silence.

At the beginning level the necessary aims and methods
appeared quite clear. What seemed chiefly to be required
were the countless rules, punishments, and fines devised
both to safeguard the students from indolence, wayward-
ness, and worldly temptations and at the same time to put
discipline into their lives. It is perhaps fair to note in
passing that these practices involved the teaching staff in
endless concern with petty problems of discipline, for the
device of turning this responsibility over to administrative
committees had not yet been found. The end result was to
breed in the faculty a sense of futility and frustration, and
not infrequently to drive the students to resentment and
rebellion. If the process strengthened character, it is to be
doubted that it did so in intended ways. The problems
engendered by this system were not to be mitigated until
undergraduate life was enriched in relatively recent times
by the development of the extra-curriculum. But there
was also concern for moral development at a higher level.
Here the responsibility fell chiefly on the president and on
his course in moral philosophy. This course was ordinarily
a combination of theology, philosophy, and social science,
at a time before the social sciences as we know them had
been separated into the various carefully articulated fields

of study now of such lively concern. The aim of the course was to set before the student the full Christian view of the world and of man's place in it, and to provide the explanations and precepts which would enable an educated man to live properly and responsibly in this world and the next. It obviously set for itself a very ambitious program.

G. P. Schmidt, in his study, *The Old Time College President,* has written of this course: "Coming as it did in the last college year, the many-sided moral philosophy course, with its broad sweep and flexible content, was admirably adapted to serve as a vehicle for whatever information and advice the president wished to transmit to his graduating classes." We are told, for example, that President Wayland of Brown, one of the most influential of early college presidents, devoted three weeks of his course to the subject of slavery, speaking sharply in favor of emancipation in 1849 at a time when a fourth of his class were southerners.

President Nott of Union College was one of those who taught such a course. Passage by passage he dissected and analyzed Lord Kames' *Elements of Criticism,* unwilling to admit Lord Kames' contention that brutes act from instinct while man can be governed by reason. Schmidt quotes President Nott as advising the students in his class: "Man seldom acts from reason. . . . If you proceed to deal with men on this supposition you will assuredly fail. . . . Men are more rational in retirement. But in society feeling rules all. In a small class now a few students might be very rational but where the class is so large, there is less reason. In the whole college there is very little reason. And if there were a thousand here there would be no reason at all." We may hope that had President Nott lived in the present era of larger college classes he would have liberalized his scale of measurement!

As the lectures proceeded, President Nott covered a multitude of subjects suggested by his theme—how to break up a mob, the best time for courtship, even the character weakness in actors caused by the fact that they must assume so many different roles in their lives. In sum, the course became, as one student remembered it, "a comprehensive study of human nature, ranging over the whole field of physical, moral and intellectual philosophy, and applied to practical use in business, politics, and religion."

Any contemporary account of such a course must inevitably be a kind of travesty, but it would be wrong to assume, because we speak a different vocabulary, that these courses were uninformed or unimportant. Students looked forward to them with high expectation, were moved by them, learned from them, remembered them, were helped and guided by them, and often tried throughout their whole subsequent careers to live up to their exacting moral demands. The love so long felt for the old-time college clearly owed a great deal to these courses. The value placed upon them in an earlier generation is suggested by the fact that when he was involved in setting up the University of Virginia Thomas Jefferson, who was certainly in most matters an enlightened and liberal man, said that the University would accept Europeans in all the professorships save one, that of moral philosophy; this was too important. He and his associates declared very frankly that they wanted "no European gospel" in this course which "gives tone and direction to the public mind."

The course in moral philosophy is really as old as the college itself. In a sense it goes back to Aristotle. It was highly developed in England, and more highly still in Scotland. It came from colleges in those countries to the new world. It was introduced into Harvard by our first president, President Dunster. It continued to be taught here in its early form perhaps as late as the time of President Kirkland. In an era of a very restricted curriculum it called attention to many things—to natural theology, philosophy, ethics, political science, economics, psychology, history, law, and international relations. It dealt with the individual, the family, and the state; with law and freedom, with practical problems of economics and government, with property rights and slavery, and with questions posed in generation after generation concerning belief and unbelief. All this in a single year. But, amidst the variety of its subject matter and its constantly shifting focus, it never lost sight of a central purpose, which was, in the words of one early president, "[to teach] men their duty and the reasons for it."

For several generations this course was taught in many colleges by men of conviction whose conviction was itself contagious. The question I would set before you today is this: where in our college has this course gone? Clearly the president does not teach it—certainly not in a baccalaureate! Nor does anyone else, by himself. But together perhaps—students, teachers, all of us, with those who have been here before us—together perhaps we do. From the beginning this course set for itself aims which cannot be taught. But they can be learned, and it is my belief that, as in an earlier day, so they continue to be learned here now.

One of the things which seems strangest to us about the old-time college is its conception of knowledge as something relatively complete, standing in need only of being learned generation after generation, rather than as something that grows and is extended, strengthened by insight,

made more subtle and complex—yes, and more alluring—
as it becomes less familiar, is enlarged and refined by inquiry and research, and ultimately given deeper and
deeper meaning. Our concern for knowledge is no less
than theirs—including knowledge about man's nature
and what can be expected of him, and us. But we view it
differently—less finally, less certainly; we think, more
subtly; certainly less confidently.

There is a further difference. We do not conceive of
minds as instruments to be sharpened but as parts of
persons—of persons capable of enrichment by experience,
and capable too, by the conscious use and enjoyment of
mind, of playing a constructive role in their own self-
development. The whole of the experience of Harvard is
intended to speak to mind. Its art and theater, its music,
its laboratories and libraries, its games and common rooms
—all those things to which students contribute so much
during the four undergraduate years; and above all—still
—its curriculum. The curriculum remains the instrument
by which the members of the faculty—now much more
numerous and clearly no less able than ever before—continue to make available to others what they have learned
of their subjects and, in their interpretations, what they
have learned of life.

Various phrases, long since abandoned because of excessive use, describe what those who pondered about education in the era of the old-time college had in mind when
they spoke of mental training. Such phrases as "sharpen
the wits," "open one's eyes," and "enlarge the mind."
Today's program is still concerned for these things. We
now believe, however, that they are to be won not from a
single course or from several courses but as they probably
were then, from the full experience of colleges like
Harvard. But this is true, if it is true, because a university

or a college is now a society, as it was then, formed by the scholar—the modern, concerned scholar—young student scholars as well as more mature ones, blood relatives of old-time counterparts, whose patience, industry, and imagination have still the power to transmute the lifeless material of scholarship into an inspiriting word.

And what of that other matter, character; more particularly, of that other matter which our predecessors called moral character? Certainly we speak very little about this. The term is suspect. We have learned too much about human motives. But the experience of Harvard, it is to be hoped, continues to help each of us, as it did those who went before us, also at this crucial point.

The old-time course in moral philosophy was intended (and I quote): "to instil into the minds of youth . . . the principles of morality and rectitude which will give them a true and happy direction in the pursuit of all public and private virtues, and by the exercise of which they may become useful to themselves, good members of society, and ornaments to their country." Perhaps this seems by modern tests too ambitious, or too shallow, too easy. We have learned, or perhaps only learned again, of depths and darknesses in the psyche and of flaws in the human will which our predecessors either did not know or chose not to speak about. These frailties seem to us to preclude easy attainment of any simple virtue such as this and many similar pronouncements seemed to envision. We rather distrust apparent virtue; it almost ceases to inspire us. But it does not follow, despite outward manifestation, that we have all become "beat" and have ceased to care.

The standards of the scholar, the mature scholar who at his best has also become a mature person, continue to impress us—his patience, honesty, industry, his sense of "standard," his sympathy, his humility, his vision of something better beyond the tawdry and the broken.

And somewhere here too it seems to me inevitable one must, as he grows, come upon an even more important matter—the serious confrontation of the question of God. Like moral character, this subject is much less frequent and much less easy in our conversations than it appears to have been to those who were here before us a hundred, two hundred, or three hundred years ago. Perhaps college age is not now the best time for it. But it would seem to me that the finest fruit of serious learning should be the ability to speak the word God without reserve or embarrassment, certainly without adolescent resentment; rather with some sense of communion, with reverence and with joy.

This is admittedly difficult—difficult if one wishes to eschew convention and speak truth. Presumably it always will be difficult, again and again. But it can be much less so than certain conventions, limitations, and pretensions in recent thought seem frequently to have made it.

It becomes man to worship. We do it less frequently and less well than we might. Dean Horton remarked in his Beecher lectures at Yale last year that "the extraordinary element in worship is that it is directed to God, whom the worshiper never sees or otherwise apprehends through perception by the senses." It is the all but universal testimony of mankind that God cannot be known in this way.

Dean Horton went further to say that "God is his own master and cannot be brought to heel by any compulsion, even the compulsion of most logical thinking." This it seems to me is a truth which must be acknowledged, even in academe. But Dean Horton then spoke of "sacramental experiences" which come to all men—or certainly to many men—of a kind which I believe most of us have had and will have. It was his point that these experiences of insight—and heightened beauty, of generosity and love, given not won, come to us from God, and that coming they both call us to worship and, calling, also supply the object and the reason for it.

It is my deepest prayer today that no one's experience of Harvard, during the long exercise of mind and concern for the problems of mind which are the stuff of living here, shall have been wholly destitute of that kind of sacramental experience of which Dean Horton spoke.

Today's Harvard and the old-time college do not look very much alike. There is the Yard, and then the great contemporary university in which the old-time Harvard College is hard to find. Indeed they have great differences. But they also have much in common—much more than the baccalaureate service. Underlying them both is concern for mind and character, and for spirit. Surely the course in moral philosophy which students have here, taught neither by professor nor president but which they have given to themselves, is no contemptible course. It is the hope of the college that it will grow in her sons, be remembered by them, be valued and ever held in honor, and that in all that befalls her sons hereafter there will be elements of beauty and knowledge, and resources of strength and renewals of faith, which might not have been there, or would have been less well developed, less certain, had they never lived here as students.

It is Harvard's hope that she will be remembered by all who shared her life—past and present—as a beloved place, hallowed both by mind and spirit, a place of learning and a source of inward strength.

* * * * * * *

WHAT MAKES A COLLEGE GOOD?

What makes a college good? The students have a good deal to do with the matter. They are implicated through their attitude, their preparation, their motivation, and through the character and degree of their participation. We have all heard that students are today much brighter than they used to be—so bright as to cause parental bewilderment at producing such progeny, and professorial terror at having to teach them. But it seems to me this kind of worry can be overdone. In many institutions the percentage of exceptionally able students is certainly greater than it was even a decade ago, and the proportion of the inept and indifferent presumably therefore less, but I cannot believe that colleges are today ministering to some radically different and superior kind of being rather than to the old familiar *homo sapiens* with all his familiar shortcomings.

What teachers still hope for from students, even the best of them when they come to college, is chiefly, and modestly, only that somewhere along the line they shall have learned to read. I do not mean by this simply to have acquired the ability to identify words and negotiate sentences. This is easy enough. But truly to read. By this I mean to interrogate significant texts, to tear them apart with the mind, understand them, rend their thoughts,

Address at the inauguration of Fred Carrington Cole as President of Washington and Lee University, Lexington, Virginia, May 7, 1960.

enter into them, and in the process possess them. This is
something else and more difficult. Perhaps it is not too
much to say that true learning can only begin—and so a
college only begin to be good—when students are at hand
who do this, and do it not simply by compulsion, but by
the incentive of self-impulse, with discrimination, and
with joy.

It is not my intention, by beginning with the students,
to imply that the faculty have no responsibility for the
merit, or lack of merit, in a college. Indeed theirs is a
frightening responsibility, for the faculty have in the first
place to be convincing exemplars of the life of learning.
It is not necessary that each member of a faculty be one
of the world's great scholars, a prestigious figure among
his specialist kind; but it is necessary that he be a scholar,
that his scholarship shall have brought him to secure
knowledge of his subject, that his knowledge be his own—
alive and growing, and not a textbook's information—and
that he have some ability, some method or artistry, to communicate both his learning and his enthusiasm for the
field of his inquiry and his sense of its importance, to
younger minds finding their way into that world il-
lumined by intellect where his own chief pleasure is found.

The faculty are under special responsibility to provide
a suitable curriculum, an instrument needed for informed
and orderly intellectual advance. And they must be able
to make of it, not an idol or a restrictive force, but a lively,
exacting, and stimulating tool. A poorly designed and inadequately staffed curriculum can fritter away intellectual
energy on a wide scattering of elementary courses which
simply skim the surfaces of their subjects. It can paralyze
thought by setting before students only shallow syntheses,
broadly inclusive; the tidy formulations of neat but un-
original and not very penetrating minds. The matter is

made worse if these courses are presented dully and routinely without enthusiasm. Courses of this kind, taught in such a way, cannot provoke but will rather stifle interest and imagination, for they merely present to memory what Whitehead so rightly called inert ideas.

Then again, a curriculum can frustrate true learning by imposing requirements which constantly force the student to turn his thoughtful attention from one subject to another in order to broaden his mind, as if—healthful as are change and variety—it were not more important to seek penetration and the kind of sustained intellectual inquiry which can go forward only on the basis of knowledge. And there are curricula too limited and impoverished to meet the variety of interests in a lively undergraduate group. And there are curricula too confining, and others put together for too narrowly specialized professional purposes, attractive and liberating as they may be for some, which prove totally inadequate for the mature needs of the growing, pressing, curious minds of a fully active undergraduate population. Above all: whatever the curriculum, if the college is to be good, its work must have a sense of relevance and importance, a feeling that it connects with large ideas and activities. Somehow it must awaken, provoke, challenge each student to do independent work at every stage—not necessarily self-consciously "original" work, but something which goes markedly beyond getting a lesson for its own sake, and in doing so simply memorizing another's outline.

There are other requirements if a college is to be good: the books themselves, the libraries, laboratories and their equipment, the places to study, to discuss and dispute, the residences and classrooms, the places to eat together, and the very people necessary to manage the physical plant— all those are essential to a college. There is need also for *beautiful* physical attributes, for these, as certain of your buildings here, have a special power and place. And reinforcing all these requirements must be the people who take thought for the whole—informed and devoted trustees concerned to find the means, the very great means, to support the indispensable catalysts, the select individuals with intellectual contributions to make. There is need for many who will work diligently in various ways adequately to nourish the life of the intellectual community which is the college.

The community itself is of crucial importance. College life at its best has about it a very special quality owing in part to the student and his time of life but also especially to the people who live in colleges and bring to them their special concerns and activities. For a lively college community creates for itself a kind of life which contrasts sharply with that of other places in the values it serves, and also to a degree, in the intensity with which it serves them. Compounded of thought and feeling—unusual, deeply fused with expectancy and aspiration—through the totality of its experience a good college community catches and charms not all, but always some, enthralled victims who, once caught, can never quite forget nor ever deny the experience.

Testimony to the special quality of college communities and to the charm of their life at its best has been offered by many individuals. For an earlier generation certain novels of Willa Cather's seemed to many to capture its essence. The college world which lived in Miss Cather's memory and to which she returned again and again in her writing was that of the University of Nebraska in the early 1890's. Measured by today's standards it was a very unimpressive college world, but for her it had all the essentials.

Claude Wheeler in *One of Ours,* Jim Burden in *My Ántonia*—for these and others of her heroes, "going to college" proved to be a profound, at first almost a shattering, but certainly always an awakening, experience. Coming for the most part from small towns, they moved into a world suffused with learning which possessed a range of interests greater by far than anything they had known before. There they underwent a kind of magic remaking, felt for the first time the excitement of intellectual experience, genuine and lively, and came at once to wonder how their former blind existence could ever have been mistaken for life.

The broadened view and new excitement which gripped them did not always derive from experiences in classrooms. Nor necessarily from experiences with members of the faculty—though sometimes they did. In the case of Jim Burden, his awakening was chiefly owed to Gaston Cleric, the head of the Latin Department, who, as presented by Miss Cather, was an accomplished and inspiring teacher, bringing to life antique stories otherwise immobile, lost in shadow. Already in the early 1890's the University of Nebraska had attracted to its faculty at least a few men of profound learning who had the ability to inspire. This is the chief point. For above all a good college must provide inspiration. If its communal life is dull or cheap, if students, faculty, and other participants in its community do not create an enticing, appealing life, based in knowledge and touched with aspiration, true learning can never there take place, nor a bright mind come alive and begin to grow.

Miss Cather had known such a world, had lived the experience. She wrote engagingly about it. Her heroes going to college entered this world, met new ideas, new kinds of people, and interests and concepts of value never before imagined by them. Excited by these experiences, they walked and talked, read and thought, argued and debated, saw beauty and excitement, and lived vividly in a new and completely captivating world of deepened thought and intense feeling.

This new world was essentially a world of ideas, and of people who differed from any the heroes had ever met because they cared about ideas and found in them substance for their lives. Miss Cather herself had met such people in Lincoln, people who kept alive in their homes a knowledge and interest in old-world cultures. By the vitality and range of their intellectual concerns, they presented a sharp contrast to the general run of Nebraska settlers in the pioneer period.

Experiences similar to those described by Miss Cather are, at deepest level, what brings one to college, though they cannot consciously be anticipated before they are felt. In my judgment an undergraduate college will never do its task well if it does not work such transformations in interest, awareness, and concern, and enliven knowledge within us. And the whole community must give itself to the enterprise if a college is to effect changes of this crucial kind.

The primitive college community of Miss Cather's heroes caught them up in new experience, increased their awareness, and enormously enhanced their understanding of the potential of life. Miss Cather's major interests were centered in the world of literature, the theater, and art. She cared most about people who knew and discussed books and players and authors. It is not surprising that her heroes tended to exhibit the same interests. We miss in them our present-day preoccupation with society, politics, and the developing nations of the world. But the basic point is not so much the specific foci of their interests as the new manner and degree to which the experience of college caused them to find excitement in the use of mind. It set them groping for perceived and analyzed human experience just as it bred in them dissatisfaction with the ordinary, dull, and routine. It taught them to scorn the imperceptive existence of their earlier lives and deprecate the seemingly smug contentment of the clodlike adult majority. Yet deepened experience enabled some of these heroes also later to discern value in areas where the first impact of college had raised questions.

A generation of college students subsequent to that for which Miss Cather wrote was soon to be much more intensely concerned with questions of politics and economics, and active participants in causes. Interests of this kind ebb and flow in college communities, but these particular concerns appear—happily it seems to me—to be reviving in our time. And earlier interests in art and theater, now widened and deepened, also revive. To them have been added the wonder of exploring new worlds within the cell and molecule, of searching the psyche, of examining strange cultures formerly distant but now brought close to us, of ranging from the microcosm of earth to the macrocosm of outer space. At the same time, concern for theological issues also again comes alive.

Meanwhile, a good college continues to offer membership in an exciting world of mind. Now as in Miss Cather's time it offers intellectual fellowship and breeds dissatisfaction with the shallow and ordinary, with the unexamined, with the pretentious, with the senseless, the dull, and dishonest. It tends to make a man wish to think for himself. It fills him with impatience at inertia and indifference and ancient encrustations that inhibit life, confining it in darkened places. It breeds in him hope and interest and alertness, makes him sensitive to the needs of others, helps him lessen the constraints of imperious self, puts purpose in life, and gives joy in the play of mind. It stimulates concern for things deeply felt and thought, and excites in the individual the prospect of shaping for himself a full adult experience continued in such concern.

What gives value to a college is its capacity to draw succeeding generations of young people into its manner of life by sustaining that life within its boundaries in all its liveliness and loveliness. What makes a college good, in short, is its magic power, perennially renewed, to widen experience, and in so doing to work those transformations, even exaltations, in young minds and hearts, indeed in all of us, drawing us into fuller and deeper life and engendering in us processes of learning which, when sustained, enable us later in less favorable circumstances still to care when the bloom of fresh excitement shall have passed.

As contrasted with the college world which meant so much to Miss Cather, we would want ours today to be less backward-looking, less escapist, less exclusively preoccupied with art and letters. We would want it to relate more immediately to the present great world outside the college where the issues large and small and the formative events and changes of our time are taking place. We prize detachment less highly. We hope we are less disdainful and more discriminating. And we yearn more for involvement; or at least some of us do. Play of mind, concern for people, exploration of the human heart, quickened allegiance to values beyond the ordinary and mundane—it is interests and activities of this kind, sustained in a society or community enlightened by ideas, which characterize a college alive to do its job. And it is the enlivening involvement in concerns and activities of this kind which makes it good.

* * * * * * *

THE AMERICAN UNIVERSITY
1960

THE AMERICAN UNIVERSITY is, in 1960, an astonishing institution. It addresses itself to an amazing assort-
ment of students of different ages, interests, intentions,
ambitions, and degrees of preparation. It offers instruction
to what people in other countries consider to be enormous
numbers of undergraduates pursuing courses in the arts
and sciences, and to even larger numbers at work in one
or another of a multitude of programs of professional or
semi-professional study which are often frankly and deliberately—even proudly—vocational. It must provide for
talented undergraduates and for those of little talent; for
those who work industriously and for some who scarcely
work at all. At the same time it also must meet the needs
of a large and rapidly growing number of graduate students. These too are of many different kinds—some of
them studying to become scholars, investigators, and university teachers; others (a more numerous group) preparing for professional life at an advanced level.

At the American university today there are also increasing numbers of postgraduate, or better, postdoctoral students, who come to our universities for many different
reasons from countries all over the world. And there are
other kinds of older students, not candidates for degrees,

Address for "University Day" at the University of North Carolina,
Chapel Hill, North Carolina, October 12, 1960.

to many of whom the name "student" is properly applied only in the sense that we all are—or should be—students for life. These include teachers from high schools and from colleges and universities coming back for special programs and scholars from other universities and countries who return to follow quests in special laboratories, to work with teachers who are making fresh advances in their fields, to make use of unique collections, or simply to avail themselves of the extraordinary resources and opportunity for study which a university normally provides.

There are also other older individuals—with advanced professional interests—who come to the university from branches of the military and from departments of government, from business and industry, from agriculture and journalism, from labor and medicine, and from other fields. And there are groups of people—policy makers in government and in business, labor leaders, city-planners —a considerable variety of professionals who choose to come together for longer or shorter periods of time in a university atmosphere to get what help they can from specialist professors, to learn from each other, to share their knowledge, and together to take thought concerning problems of mutual concern.

Perhaps this brief review furnishes sufficient reason for us to feel sorry for today's professors who are pulled in so many directions. The early American university served no such mishmash of people. And there is more to the story of the contemporary professor's plight. So ubiquitous and pressing is the need for expertness and so many are the members of university faculties called upon to perform the endless and multiplying variety of consultative and advisory functions in behalf of individuals and organizations—governments, businesses, professional associations here and abroad—that it would not be surprising to find at any given moment a considerable percentage of all professors and administrative officers about to go into orbit, flying in many directions on an astonishing variety of missions all over the globe. At Harvard we have at least one professor who can hardly wait to get to the moon.

Beyond the demands of teaching, advising, and instructing are the even more difficult requirements of investigation and research. Today's scholars are under necessity to occupy and explore the frontiers, and to plumb the depths of a terrain of knowledge so expanded and deepened, and now seen to be so complicated, that comparing it with the restricted fields of earlier concern makes former investigators and their preoccupations sometimes seem primitive and simple.

The view of the American university has now lifted beyond the confines of western culture to scan cultures of the whole world. Its attention to international studies has also sharply increased, broadened and deepened. Other new fields for exploration and teaching have come into being. Nuclear experimentation, defense studies, investigations in oceans and space are only a few of the fields in which rigorous work has been made possible by scholarly and technical advance. There are also some fields in which study has been made necessary by political development. And there are others—the mechanisms of business, the behavior of groups large and small, psychiatry in medicine. These, their subdivisions, and many more have captured the interest of groups of scholars and have become strongly established in the university's curricula. Discrimination of new fields of knowledge, and of new areas for intensified investigation within old fields, follows inevitably year by year with scholarly advance. Fraught with special excitement and promise at the moment are the penetrations of experimental biologists into such areas of wonder as the innermost recesses of the cell; and side by side with this and others, the continuing efforts of humanists to bring fresh light to that island universe which will always be of deepest interest to us, the human heart.

Knowledge old and new lives and is mediated through books. Within them is stored for future use the intellectual capital of the race. Again and again they serve as catalytic agents prompting fresh intellectual discovery. Without books—many books—a university could not attract, nor provide for, nor keep scholars, nor could its surrounding community grow beyond a limited and impoverished manner of life. Today the flood of books in countless languages pouring from the presses of the world, recording the experiences, hopes, discoveries, plans of peoples everywhere, is larger than ever before, and a research library to be alive must grow with this torrent. Somehow in our universities we must keep up with the full flood—not each of us with all of it, but together, dividing the burden in some sensible manner, with all that can be shown to be relevant in our broadened and broadening world of learning.

Is there now a central, dominating idea at work within this complicated institution which holds it together and in some degree directs its activity and animates its parts? Here old ideas seem no longer quite to serve.

Newman, you remember, who spoke so eloquently of "the idea of the university" a little more than a century ago—about a decade before the passage of the Morrill Land-Grant Act in this country—felt that the magic power of great teaching to elicit creative response in young minds constituted the essential university activity. His was and remains an attractive theory. It was his view that a university will discharge the full measure of its social responsibility if only it can produce in each generation a few men equipped with judicious minds. This view is made winsome by his description of several kinds of injudicious minds not unfamiliar in our time. "What is more common," he says, "than the sight of grown men talking on political or moral or religious subjects, in that offhand, idle way, which we signify by the word *unreal*? . . . Such persons have no difficulty in contradicting themselves in successive sentences, without being conscious of it. . . . Others, whose defect in intellectual training is more latent, have their most unfortunate crochets, as they are called, or hobbies, which deprive them of the influence which their estimable qualities would otherwise secure. . . . Others can never look straight before them, never see the point, and have no difficulties in the most difficult subjects. Others are hopelessly obstinate and prejudiced, and, after they have been driven from their opinions, return to them the next moment without even an attempt to explain why. Others are so intemperate and intractable that there is no greater calamity for a good cause than that they should get hold of it. . . ."

We may all agree that if universities could expunge such injudicious minds from society and substitute for them minds marked by good sense, sobriety of thought, reasonableness, candor, self-command, and steadiness of view, as Newman advocated, they would be amply justified. Any theory which produced this result would have to be held in respect. But, after centuries of higher education, opinionatedness remains with us.

For Newman, knowledge tended to be something established and familiar. It was at least familiar to cultivated people. The teacher's task was simply to stimulate young minds to pursue it. Though he paid lip service to the importance of research, by and large, like the French after the educational reforms of Napoleon or like the Russians

today he would leave the chief responsibility for research
to academies and institutes outside universities. But unlike these—certainly unlike today's Russians—in his heart
of hearts he had very little enthusiasm for any kind of
research beyond that quiet reading for the attainment of
wisdom which has been traditionally associated, with
varying degrees of justification, with the scholar's study.
It was his view that if a university's objective were scientific or philosophical discovery it would have no need of
students. He seems in this regard to have had almost no
appreciation of the notion that research might improve
teaching—an idea which chiefly motivated our pioneers in
the higher "higher learning" who labored zealously in the
closing decades of the nineteenth century to establish university as contrasted with college education in this country.
For this reason it was easy for him then to argue in a circle
that since students were indispensable, obviously teaching, not research, was the university's aim.

If there has been a single dramatic change within our
universities during the past two decades it is in the enormous increase in the amount of research now done within
them. I can suggest the nature of this, if I may, by citing
a statistic or two with which I am familiar from the experience of Harvard. Twenty-five years ago Harvard had
only 88 purely research appointments; last year there were
876. Twenty-five years ago Harvard's Department of
Chemistry spent less than $100,000 on research; last year
this department alone spent over a million dollars for this
purpose. The amount spent for research in the Harvard
Medical School in 1934 was $222,000. By 1959 this
School's annual budget for research had risen to more
than five million dollars. These figures make no allowance
for inflation nor do they tell anything of the worth of
results achieved. The research done could of course—al-

though I am confident it is not—be trivial, misdirected, unimaginative, and pedestrian. But the amount spent at least suggests a very substantial shift in interest, in aim, and in practice of a kind which has occurred in department after department, in university after university, since the early years of World War II. Indeed the amount spent on research in all our universities rose by more than 2,600 per cent from $27,000,000 in 1939–40 to $734,000,-000 in 1957–58.

In a sense this gargantuan growth of research in our universities represents the triumph of a theory planted in them at the time of their second, true beginnings to which I referred a moment ago. This theory did not come to us from the British educational practice which Newman knew, loved, and eloquently described, but rather from a concept of higher education developed in Germany in the nineteenth century. The difference between the two views can be explained in part by the fact that the German university was peopled by students older than Newman's undergraduates. Their ages were usually from twenty to twenty-five. But a much more basic point of cleavage is that the German university looked first to the professor rather than to the student, and, even more fundamentally, back of the professor to the world of knowledge.

German theory did not conceive the world of knowledge as a static world, but rather as a world steadily being discovered: one might almost say, seemingly being visibly created by the combined efforts of professors. At the turn of the century, Friedrich Paulsen, one of the most articulate writers on German higher education, summed up the case for the German university in this fashion: "The [German] university's teachers were the true exponents of scientific research," he said, "and its students the scholars of the future."

During the nineteenth century the German university reached a level of accomplishment to which other universities had not yet even considered to aspire. Its triumphs in its aim to advance knowledge were everywhere the glory and the envy of the academic world. In time almost all non-German institutions of higher learning which were alive came to feel its influence and then sought to make themselves over in its image. Certainly our leading and most ambitious American institutions did. And we continue to honor this German ideal. But we were never able—perhaps never really wanted—to serve only this ideal. Always what appear to have been rather typically American considerations of utility exercised a complicating and withstanding hold on our hearts and minds.

There were voices in our country calling for practical education, for instruction in the agricultural, mercantile, and mechanical arts, long before the passage of the Morrill Act—those of Franklin, Jefferson, Wayland, among others. Harvard had a scientific school as early as 1847, and it was not the first of its kind. All along there had been iconoclasts arguing that higher education should be adapted to the needs of what Ezra Cornell called "the industrial and productive classes of society," and all along their voices have been heard—on balance, we believe, to advantage. This has contributed to make today's American university the hybrid creature it is.

The question I pose is whether within this curious, multiform, overworked—but advancing, even erupting— institution there is now any central idea or concept to hold the American university together. Despite all its service functions, despite all the distractions occasioned by demands from many kinds and conditions of people, despite the variety of interests it serves, the extent of the field of knowledge with which it wrestles, and its incredible array of enterprises, it is and remains, before all else and in the midst of all else, a community for learning— a community in which all participants continue stead- fastly to hold learning in high regard.

Long ago, speaking of German universities, Paulsen said there was not one of them which had not sent out men who became distinguished scientists and others who played other important roles in the developing life of their country. He said that because of this each university har- bored within it a sense of history and of high endeavor, and that everyone who came into the university com- munity was encompassed by its atmosphere of historic life and took something of it with him when he left. Cannot we say the same?

Earlier Savigny spoke, with the aristocratic overtones of his time, concerning the power for inspiration and moti- vation which lies within university communities. He said that the universities' value lay not in "the perfect learning of their teachers or in the ever-growing learning of their students"—"If we should name this as their distinction," he said, "a mirror would often need to be held before us to our shame"—but rather that in them "there is given a scheme, wherein every important educational talent finds its development . . . through which every advance of sci- ence finds easy and rapid entrance, [and] by which is made easy the recognition of the higher calling of ex- ceptional men, and in which even to the poorer existence of more limited natures a higher sense of life is imparted."

In another idealistic passage, making no allowance for degrees of merit, Newman spoke of the university as "an assemblage of learned men zealous for their own sciences, and rivals of each other, brought by familiar intercourse and for the sake of intellectual peace, to adjust together the claims and relationships of their respective subjects of investigation, and to learn to respect, consult, and aid each other." Though scholars today often appear to pursue separate ways within universities—quite unaware of their colleagues' existence, certainly without all quarrels adjusted—still by and large they all are, and know they are, working in a common vineyard. They know that it is not their specialties but "learning" in its double sense—both as a constantly developing field of knowledge and as an intellectual process—which they have in common. The connecting link for all within the university remains learning thus understood, a compact of knowledge, effort, and hope.

In America the university grew from the college, and the university continues to have an undergraduate college within it. I hope it always will. It is the function of the college to create a world of mind where the accumulated intellectual experience of the race is held in honor and kept viable. It provides a map and a guide to the realm of knowledge, and admits students presumably capable and interested in exploring that map. Admittedly these students often have other aims in mind when they come— aims both social and vocational. But if the work of college teaching is well performed, and if the community properly speaks to the needs of undergraduates, the inadequacy of early ideas will be made good and some measure of pride and joy in learning instilled before these students depart.

But larger than the college is the university. Here must go on learning at its highest, best, and most inclusive— and discovery in learning. Today the activity of learning breaks out in a multitude of unanticipated and often untried directions. Wherever the affairs of men call for intellectual analysis, discrimination, criticism, formulation, concern—here must the university follow. The important point is that we must continue steadily to refuse ever to do this on easy, unintellectual, or cheapened terms.

And so at the end I return to my question: Is there a central dominating idea enlivening the American university today? The answer is, most certainly, yes. For such an idea is formed in the devotion to learning which permeates the whole community and in the recognition of learning's importance for a full manner of life.

Undaunted by repeated misunderstanding from outside, undeterred by confusion, some uncertainty, and failures within, lively and free the American university continues to pursue its high aim, stronger today, better staffed, better equipped for its task, more relevant, more vital and more central to us than ever before. It has moved into new fields and is constantly being called upon for more and more services. It has been receiving increased support—and needs more. It is steadily winning for its work a larger percentage of the nation's talent. So vastly has it grown and multiplied its purposes that at a quick glance it might appear to have become a wholly new kind of institution. But it remains an extended and improved version of what it has always been—a community for learning.

Our task is to keep the American university—here and elsewhere—a place of lively learning. For the influence of this remarkable institution is now called upon to spread beyond these shores, as our country grows in power and place and our scholars, recruited from everywhere, join with scholars everywhere in the endless pursuit of truth.

It is not too much to say in the autumn of 1960 that the American university's full mission has only scarcely begun.

* * * * * * *

HARVARD'S PURPOSE

THE DUTIES of the President of Harvard are defined by statute. Among them is the responsibility "to direct the official correspondence of the University." I discovered quite early that this apparently innocent item in the list of the President's duties is in fact a kind of joker, for one does not need to be President of Harvard long to learn that there are times when this obligation, frequently pleasant, can be more onerous than all the others combined.

What, for example, do I say in response to a letter like this?

So then I asked myself why should I support an institution which lends itself so heavily to teaching the form of government in which I do not believe and to which I am unalterably opposed. Granted, freedom to think and reasonable academic latitude is desirable, but when a whole Harvard department, dealing with our way of life, is so strongly promoting measures leading to totalitarianism, it would seem I would be weakminded to support it.

How do I reply when the image of Harvard in the mind of the writer of this letter, and of others of his kind, bears almost no resemblance to the Harvard I live with, believe in, and work to strengthen and advance?

Address at the annual meeting of the Harvard Alumni Association in the Harvard Yard on the afternoon of Commencement Day, June 15, 1961.

This particular consideration raises a general question which I repeatedly ask myself: What can I say or do to ensure that there be a reasonably accurate image of Harvard abroad in the land; that there be at least a moderate congruence between what men think of Harvard—especially, what Harvard men think of Harvard—and the facts?

Admittedly it is not easy to say what Harvard is. But is it what some one person, or perhaps several persons serving particular interests, say it is? Of course not! Is it what newspapers caught up in current events and trying by shorthand methods to communicate with mass audiences imply at some heated moment that it is? Of course not!

There are more than 120,000 living Harvard alumni. In any given year now there are thirteen thousand students in residence here, and almost five thousand officers and teachers. From time to time some few of these speak out publicly in a way to attract attention, but the great majority exercise their influence in quieter ways and by less spectacular actions. Who is to tell what this multitude really thinks, believes, and wants for and of Harvard? Surely there are almost as many Harvards as there are Harvard men.

It would be interesting if we could ascertain what each of you knows intimately of Harvard today, of what her influence is, of what she is saying or trying to say to the young people who live and work and aspire here—if we could observe how far your thinking about Harvard is based on knowledge and how far it is based rather on fancy or memory or report, even on stereotype, than on actuality. I do not know, but the burden of what I want to say today is to make a plea that all of you—especially any among you who have drifted into doubt about Har-

vard—will make a conscientious effort to eschew hearsay
and innuendo, take a fresh look, update your image of
Harvard, and try to see this university as it truly is.

Harvard is a complex, lively, and involved institution.
Now as always she includes many kinds and conditions of
people—people of different interests, views, and opinions;
and this grows increasingly so, the more the University
becomes a world institution. But this is good, for diversity
of opinion makes one think. As much as anything it may
set one on the path toward truth. But never has Harvard
tried to teach a single narrow orthodoxy in any field, nor
does she now. From the time our first president, Henry
Dunster, was dismissed for unorthodoxy, it has been her
chief purpose to call men to think for themselves. Again
and again there has been difficulty about this. Henry
Dunster did not meet the conditions of the Massachusetts
theocracy, but Harvard respected him for his courage and
conviction, and in time named a House for him. Harvard
still honors courage, conviction, and independent thought
in her main and central thrust. As William James said in
his much quoted address at Commencement fifty-eight
years ago this month, "The day when Harvard shall stamp
a single fast and hard type of character upon her children
will be that of her downfall."

This university—as all universities insofar as they measure up to the great ideal they serve—admires honesty,
decency, integrity, knowledge, subtleties of mind, the
fundamental importance of thought, and responsible action based on thought. These have always been Harvard's
directing aims. They still are. Some individuals, having
been given more imagination, or being less confused by
the distorting mechanisms of imperious selfhood, may
serve these ends better than others, but in some degree,

insofar as she has helped to shape us, Harvard enlists us all in their defense.

Harvard has had a great deal of publicity lately, good and bad. This has given birth to a new flood of *ex cathedra* statements about her from a multitude of individuals who know too little of what they speak. Many of these individuals because of their own personal beliefs concerning some viewpoint taken by a Harvard graduate, a Harvard teacher, or a Harvard student would make general charges against the whole institution, condemning it to perdition, or in the case of an occasional unhappy graduate, at least to exclusion from his charity and his affection.

Let me hasten to add that it would not be fair to the author of the letter I have quoted to classify him with the completely disenchanted Harvard public. He has been a friend of Harvard medicine in this year when we are raising large sums to strengthen the program of the Medical School and the affiliated teaching hospitals. This correspondent will give to Harvard medicine, and we are grateful to him for that. Harvard medicine deserves everyone's support. But he does not care to give any money to the University for general purposes, because he is convinced there is a "socialistic slant" here. He suspects the Economics Department of fostering this, and he says he will withhold his gifts so long as his money might be used "to bring along a new crop of free thinkers." What troubles me here is simply that his view of Harvard and mine could be so completely out of phase.

The notion that any department at Harvard is a tight-knit little group trying to impose a point of view seems to me utterly fantastic. I am confident I now know these departments as well as anyone outside them can. There are almost thirty of them in the College; and there are at least a hundred subordinate divisions indicating special fields of knowledge in the whole University. In my experience almost every one of them is made up of such a variety of individuals, is so splintered in its interests, assumptions, and fundamental convictions, that it is little short of a minor miracle whenever in a controversial matter anything approximating a clearly defined majority point of view can be identified and made to prevail. How, knowing this and wrestling every day with the problems presented by such diversity, do I reply to letters like the one with which I began these comments?

To see this problem in better perspective let me take a moment to read an excerpt from a report of a Harvard Visiting Committee. The gentlemen of this committee stated that they

continue this year, as in previous years, unable to appreciate the wisdom and propriety of what seems to them an entirely partial and one-sided instruction. For the United States it is a vital issue that is being fought out . . . which may involve the welfare of the country for generations to come. In this conflict Harvard College has, in their opinion, practically taken sides as decidedly as if she constituted a political body instead of an educational institution. . . .

This Visiting Committee, like the author of the letter quoted, was speaking of economics at Harvard (or rather of political economy as it was then called), but its attack was directed at the department of Bowen, Dunbar, and Taussig, men whose views we would today term at least very moderate, if not conservative. The report quoted was written seventy-three years ago!

In my judgment those who today try to imply an overarching Keynesian (whatever they mean by that!) or even a Marxist slant to our teachings in this subject know

neither Harvard nor the subject of economics in our time.
Yet it is possible that many Harvard men do not know of
Professor Mason's studies in economic development or of
his enormous helpfulness as economic adviser to emerging
nations, of Professor Leontief's input-output studies, of
Professor Meyer's concern with quantitative economics
and econometrics, of Professor Kuznets' research on cycles
and economic growth, of Professor Gerschenkron's studies
in economic history, of Professor Schelling's experimental
studies of rational economic decisions in conflict and uncertainty, of Professor Dunlop's work in wages, prices, and
labor relations, of Professor Haberler's preoccupation
with international trade and economic policy, or of Professor Overton Taylor's considerations of economic
thought, including his notable historical essay on *The
Classical Liberalism, Marxism and the Twentieth Century,* which some regard as a minor classic. Can anyone
seriously charge that these men and the others in their
department are subverting the American way of life? And
can one seriously charge the same of the University as a
whole, taking note of its program in history, government,
public administration and social relations, and its far-
reaching effort in business, which is almost completely
directed toward making the private enterprise system continue to work effectively and beneficially in a very difficult
world? And then we are only taking into consideration
one small part of the University's activity—without noting the multitudinous and incredibly wonderful work carried on here in the arts, humanities, and sciences.

Let me say quite frankly—even bluntly—that someone
here is living in a never-never land. Is it I or my corres-
pondents of the kind quoted? I hope you will excuse the
apparent lack of modesty, but in this important matter of
trying to define what Harvard in fact today is, I can only

say that it is not I who am misinformed. And it is because
of the deep conviction I have gained of the essential right-
ness of Harvard's present orientation and enterprise, after
eight years of careful inquiry following almost twenty
years of absence, that I dare to express the hope that all
Harvard men who have felt even the slightest uncertainty
concerning this issue will care enough about the College's
enduring purpose to look into the matter again, rigor-
ously, for themselves. If you will do this—and cease to
talk about or be put off by caricatures—I am confident
you will discover, or rediscover, Harvard's central and
abiding character, will be filled again with admiration
and enthusiasm for it, and will find a new determination
to help Harvard on her way.

Our world is full of divergencies of opinion and unlimited perils. Granted. And this has made us all abnor-
mally apprehensive. But surely the way to cope with this
situation is not to begin by saying there is some simple,
easily recognizable right to which we must adhere, and
that all other views are wrong. Nor, let me add in fairness
to my critic, is there any need to assume or even acquiesce
in the view that any single individual who talks most frequently, or most conspicuously, or most assertively must
necessarily therefore be right, or even in any degree rep-
resentative. We all learned in the first discussion class we
ever attended that this is not so. Somewhere underlying
the diversity of a great university is an integrity proof
against all idiosyncratic and partisan views.

Our world is full of divergencies of opinion, and so is
Harvard. Each autumn an almost limitless number of
different points of view is brought into our community.
Individuals come here from different regions, from different races, from different economic groups, representing
many of the differences that world culture in the second

half of the twentieth century can furnish. Even more
basically each autumn our new recruits include all the
different kinds of personality the good Lord provides,
with all the differences resulting from multivariant home
situations often reflecting distortions in human relations
wrought by failures through generations. From such a
variety of points of origin do we come. Then, becoming
Harvard men, we all join to sing praise to Veritas, though
we should acknowledge in all humility that if ever we
were to stop to inquire precisely what Veritas means, in
all probability such a hassle would break out among us as
our reasonably well-mannered community has rarely seen.
In such a situation, Harvard moves in and tries again to
speak to the individual human being—the completely
fresh individual human person—to say something to him
of integrity, truth, discrimination, of caring and concern,
and also of the beauty and power of tradition. It is not
surprising if we emerge with much variety and difference
from our experiences of Harvard. It is a miracle that we
come out with as much agreement as we do.

What is the sum of these few brief remarks? It is simply
that in my judgment there is one thing Harvard men must
be agreed about. This is the recognition that truth is not
something easily identifiable or simply stated, and that,
this being so, those other qualities for which we all care
so much—integrity, concern, and courage—these qualities
make serious demands for understanding upon us all.

Harvard is a magnificent institution and has been for
most of her thirteen quarter-centuries. God willing, she
will be for even more full centuries. I am glad that so
many alumni have come back to visit the College this
week. I hope you have liked what you have seen here, and
I hope you have seen abundant evidence that we are not
in the slightest degree a "subversive" institution. I hope,

more seriously, you have seen reason to believe that as a present leader among universities in the world Harvard continues to stand for those high principles for which she stood as a founder of the higher learning on this continent three hundred and twenty-five years ago, and that she is now working patiently, industriously, imaginatively, and powerfully in a common enterprise with many to extend the influence of those principles around the globe.

Again and again I feel at a loss as to how to reply to letters like the one with which I began. I call on each of you for help. Faulty images of Harvard do exist in certain areas and communities in this country, and in many individual minds. So come back to Cambridge whenever you can. Stay long enough to see what the present facts are. For when you have done this, it is my hope you will want, with renewed faith in Harvard and having found fresh inspiration from her, to go out again to join in the endless task to get her mission understood.

* * * * * * *

THE EXPECTATIONS OF
THE UNIVERSITY

A university is inevitably shaped in some degree by the expectations which confront it. What students seem most to want from their universities is knowledge—perhaps more accurately training, or even, if we are to be completely honest, only the appearance of university education—so that they may be able to compete for remunerative jobs in an urban, technological society. From the point of view of the governments which foster universities, struggling to maintain or advance their nations' positions in a revolutionary world, applied science for the sake of military safety and material growth seems chiefly to be desired.

This is obviously an oversimplification. There are many other forces at work on universities: the need for better measures of public health, for example, and for a broad range of social as opposed to narrowly economic and military improvements. More important, there are students and teachers in universities in all countries who care for liberal education for its own sake, and increasing numbers devoted to the advance of knowledge. These, always too few everywhere, are the people who, having caught a glimpse at a university of the beauty of disinterested learning and felt the excitement of intellectual discovery, can

Convocation Address at the University of Delhi, New Delhi, India, November 25, 1961.

never thereafter quite put them out of mind or cease to care for them. But a quick look at universities today—almost everywhere—suggests that the urgent contemporary problems of economic growth, industrial development, land reform, health, improved administration, labor organization, social need and military advantage increasingly direct and perhaps even compel the enterprise of universities. Unquestionably the everyday world of practical necessity has moved in forcibly upon the institutions of higher learning.

A year ago, it was my good fortune to attend the third quinquennial meeting of the International Association of Universities in Mexico City. This was my first direct experience with this association. For me it was an extraordinarily illuminating and stimulating occasion. The purpose of the meeting was to consider the present situation of the university in the world. Representatives of more than 350 universities from more than threescore countries in all parts of the globe came together for this assembly.

What struck me at the outset of the assembly was the widespread domain throughout the world over which the university now exerts or is beginning to exert her influence.

A second realization borne in upon me was how similar are the problems of universities wherever these institutions may be located. There are universities of great antiquity in the Association's membership, and also young ones, complex and comparatively simple ones, large and small ones, strong and weak ones; and yet the major themes of the conference seemed in at least some degree to be relevant for all.

We spent time at this assembly discussing the proper relationship of the university with the state. Is the university an instrument of state? Should it be? Is it wholly independent? Does it have goals of its own, goals different from those of the state? If so, how is it to pursue them? We found agreement and disagreement among ourselves on these questions.

It was part of my education to discover that what some would call "the Western view" in this matter is not everyone's view. My association is with an American university which prides itself on being private. What this term means is that we do not depend in a large degree upon either the state or the federal government for financial support. I should add at once, however, that the number of institutions of higher learning in the United States seriously independent of financial assistance from government is steadily becoming less. Harvard, one of the strongest of America's private universities, now receives about a fifth of her income annually from the federal government. Ours is a mixed situation. But the nature of the mix continues for us to be an issue of enormous importance.

I gather from my experience in Mexico City that this problem is also of concern to faculties and administrative officers in practically all countries of the free world, wherever the tradition of the university, as an institution with responsibility for establishing its own policies, is still observed. Though there are areas in the world where this is held to be an old-fashioned and mistaken notion, ours is not one of them, nor I take it, is yours. Universities and governments are now closely associated in all countries, and must be for the health of each. But we and you continue to assert that the purposes of a university are not necessarily identical with or to be comprehended within those of government.

We at Harvard are rooted in our nation, and are proud to be. We sympathize with our country and her aims. We want to be of assistance to her government, especially whenever she is beset with extraordinarily formidable and urgent difficulties as seems now almost constantly to be the case. In every generation we have given people to our government's service. This was true throughout our long colonial period; it has been increasingly so in the time of the republic, from before the presidency of John Adams to the presidency of John Kennedy. We hope this will continue to be the case. No career has greater appeal for many of Harvard's ablest sons in each generation than that of devoted public service. But we have always held that we serve our government best by remaining a university in our deepest understanding of the university's true nature. It is our wish to be of help, but we are fiercely determined not to be controlled by government, or to have our central activities finally directed by considerations, however important to government, which do not seem to us consistent with the university's basic, grand design. It was deeply encouraging to me to find that university people in most other countries feel the same.

I turn now to a second problem of widespread concern in the third assembly of the world's universities. I suspect you have been talking recently about Sir Charles Snow's "two cultures," as we have. There seems to be a lively concern in universities everywhere lest the world's current preoccupation with science, the need for science, and the power of science effect a monstrous distortion within the fabric of learning. There is world-wide worry among university people that a conjunction of material need and scientific triumph has set loose in contemporary society a force which now poses a serious threat to humane values. Surely there is reason for such concern.

Again I was reassured to discover that this worry, very pressing in the minds of many of us in the West, is by no means exclusively ours. Many in other countries appear to be as troubled about this development as we are, and apparently for very similar reasons. We have not yet fully assessed the difficulty. Certainly we have not yet found answers to it. Nor, I gather from the discussions I heard in Mexico City, have others. The impact of science and technology has far from run its course. But surely it is gain that we are all coming to a clearer realization of the fact that the advance of applied science is not necessarily a complete blessing. The trouble of course is not with science, but only with the use we make of science. But I am confident it is your deep hope, as it is ours, that the scientist as human will presently far outstrip the scientist who is simply the builder of a more efficient tool.

A third subject for discussion in Mexico City was the frightening problem presented today to the universities of all countries by increasing numbers of students. More and more people are qualified and wish to come to universities. At the same time our increasingly complex civilization needs more and more individuals (if not everywhere so rapidly as one might wish) who have had one or another of the various kinds of training which only universities can provide. So the press goes on and will continue. In face of this situation even the most fiercely independent among us are beginning to look to national governments for financial help to cope with the unprecedented, enormous responsibility presented to us.

There are more than four million young people enrolled in hundreds of colleges and universities in the United States this autumn. I remember from my own experience as an administrative officer in education when we in the United States thought a college population of a million and a half was very large. Now we expect even heavier pressure to come upon us in the decade ahead, for, large as is the present college population, the numbers of students in secondary schools in the United States are proportionately much larger, and there are markedly larger numbers following behind them in the elementary schools. We are all very much concerned to find places, facilities, and enough teachers to cope with these numbers without making concessions in standards.

But in this matter India's difficulties appear to be vastly greater than ours, and India has our sympathy as she endeavors to cope with them. I had thought before coming to India that we had developed at Berkeley in California, in New York City, in one or two other places, universities of inordinate size, and with others have often worried about how a university can survive in its essential character under the impact of increasing enrollment. Where are the teachers to be found? More important, where are the creative research scholars to be found in sufficient numbers to keep learning alive and growing so that instruction will lead naturally and gradually into the life of mind, and not become rote learning? Where the facilities, laboratories and libraries, hostels and studies?

Now I find that even very large universities in the United States are made to appear small when the numbers of their students are compared with some of India's, and the concomitant difficulties in India are proportionately the more. But all of us already need added resources to turn our existing institutions into more vibrant, more imaginative, more influential communities of learning. Now, everywhere, even before we have quite learned to do well with the students we have, we are faced with the discouraging prospect of having to cope with many, many more.

Some of the universities of the world are stronger than others; some older; some younger. They exhibit a wide variety of emphases. Some fit in this category and some in that. All today are beset by a multitude of similar problems, insistent, complex, seemingly almost insoluble because of their magnitude and intractability. Where in all this do we who care about universities find hope?

Many of today's universities are relatively young. Most have been established within the last hundred years. Yet all share in an age-old tradition. New institutions of higher learning in so far as they are universities are necessarily born in this tradition, are called to serve it, find their basic purpose and their nourishment in it.

From the beginning, wherever it has appeared, the university has been called upon for proximate aims; at the same time it has also always been devoted, in its innermost resolve, to relentless pursuit of truth—never, finally, to national, sectarian, or any kind of limited interest, but only to truth itself. We recognize that the truth the university seeks has, or should have, a moral as well as an intellectual component. We agree with some of the university's recent critics that it is not sufficient for modern man to know, but that he must also be and do. Despite the sophistries of this age, we are not prepared to concede that truth thus understood is to be identified with interests of state.

Universities are made aware daily of practical concerns. In our era there is no turning away or escape from such demands. All countries have an accelerating need for scientists, engineers, technicians, administrators of many kinds, health officers, lawyers, business leaders, and most important, teachers and research workers. Where are these to come from, if not from universities? Surely it is the university's role to meet demands of this kind. In the present new dynamic period of the world's history, peoples and nations have need of innovators as never before. They honor universities for the capacities they have for service

of this kind, and want them. The university, weak as it is
—young as it is—must respond.

But beyond all immediately practical considerations,
there is needed, deep within our university communities,
an animating conviction that what ultimately matters
among men is learning itself, quickened and brought to
full life in individual minds and through them dissemi-
nated as a force for good—for moral good as well as for
technical advance—throughout society.

The charm and the appeal of humane learning, the
pursuit of arts and letters, and of the sciences, is not exclusively for utilitarian ends—rather first for joy of the
chase. The important result is extension of the domain of
mind in an imperfect world. We in the universities are
joined together in this task. It is this vision with its at-
tendant responsibility which animates our universities,
providing a bond for community within each, and drawing us all together.

Today formidable difficulties divide the peoples and
the nations of the world. Within each country there are
serious obstacles in the way of social and economic advances required for quick realization of hopes for a better
world. Nowhere has adequate attention yet begun to be
paid to the more serious questions concerning the spiritual
dimensions in the lives of people being drawn into increasingly complex, technological urban masses. When we
look out upon the confusion, the conflicting purposes, the
hostilities, the self-seeking, the ignorance, the poverty and
wanton deception which everywhere keep us from our
dreams, it must seem at times beyond the power of men to
resolve these difficulties. And yet we cannot let our wills
be paralyzed.

Fortunately there is another side to the ledger. Con-

spicuous on it is a great network of universities—many of
them only very recently established, all at least beginning
to be marked by new ferment—which now encircles the
globe. Though these are of many kinds, at their best they
all serve a common end.

The university as we know it today is nowhere much
more than a hundred years old. In a real sense it has
scarcely yet begun its work in the world; it is still only
readying itself for the task. It is a university's role to help
a nation make full use of the talent it is given. As yet we
do this everywhere only very imperfectly. In so far as there
are more individuals in all countries who have the capacity for fuller development and the potentiality for making
constructive contributions to their countries' social advance than are now being served by them, our universities
cannot be said yet to have measured up to their full opportunity. In so far as universities fail to be lively communities for learning, they fall short. But there is ground
for hope in our beginnings. Today there are universities
in all countries, and in all universities clusters of scholars
held together by sincere devotion to the achievements of
mind. These groups seek to quicken the imaginations of
succeeding generations of the gifted young, drawing them
into an age-old enterprise. So knowledge and civilization
advance.

Learning's hold on our world has always been precarious, and it is today, despite the arrogance to which we
have been inclined by growing mastery in the physical
order. But learning's final and most important victories
are not to be won in this area, even less in the service of
the surface demands of the industrial, urban, technological and dynamic societies developing in the modern world.
Their more important victories will be won only as learn-

ing brings light into the dark recesses of the human soul and begins to effect a redeemed order of relationship among men.

Three years ago, when Prime Minister Nehru spoke at the University of Delhi, he made a striking comparison between Old Delhi and New Delhi. In their differences and yet their innate similarity he found "an epitome of India's history with its succession of glory and disaster, and its great capacity to absorb many cultures and yet remain itself." I was deeply impressed by this allusion, and it seemed to me as apt in speaking of the ideals of universities as it is of our hope for the men and women who teach at them, study at them, and go out into the world from them.

For, regardless of surrounding perils which man has created for himself, regardless of the cruelty of his actions and the crassness of his standards, regardless of his tragedy and suffering, man ever seeks to rise above his weaknesses. There is within him the urge to create, to build, to become a part of the infinite. In his imperfection he has been the author of glorious works of sculpture, painting, architecture, literature, drama, and music. Yet nowhere does the collective humanity of mankind express itself more magnificently than in the association of minds which we call a university.

There are many recent American graduates of American colleges who feel, as Indians no doubt do, frustrated because of difficulties in the way of living decently, humbly, and bravely, and see no readily accessible outlet for their urge to build. But they too have shared an experience of learning and the companionship which comes from association with others of similar high ideals. Happily they, you, and college graduates everywhere form an en-

nobling supranational fraternity which, despite the dangers and frustrations of our life on earth, will strive to
extend—through a common respect, knowledge, and conviction—the university's influence for human betterment
and peace.

* * * * * * *

THE FRAGILE CHAIN

In November 1961 I stood on a Commencement platform in Delhi, India, before a large and happy throng of Indian students, their families and friends, to make the official convocation address to the three thousand candidates for university degrees. Although the surroundings were strange to me, there were familiar aspects in the occasion. For one thing, I was acquainted with the University of Delhi's Chancellor, the distinguished Brahmin philosopher Dr. Sarvepalli Radhakrishnan, who was then Vice-President and is now President of the Republic of India. For another, the size of the university and the number of its candidates for degrees were comparable to the size and number at a graduation ceremony in my own university, Harvard.

But in most other features the circumstances were quite different; and although there is a fellowship which embraces educated men all over the world, I could not help feeling a sense of inadequacy in Delhi in presuming to talk to young people with quite different backgrounds and experiences from my own. I had never been in India before and had no idea what an American should attempt to say in such circumstances. What could I say to an alien generation in an alien land at a crucial moment in their lives—one of special significance—when they were about

Commencement address at Morehouse College, Atlanta, Georgia, June 5, 1962.

to take off from a familiar environment and a known set
of circumstances for another, strange, unknown, and
bristling with difficulties? What could I say there?

The life of a student in India is much more difficult
than anything we know in this country. Lack of material
resources hampers most of the students at every turn. An
overwhelming majority of them live at home, if they have
homes, in conditions—by any standards we know—of miserable poverty. Often they have too little to eat, very little
to wear, almost never any money to spend on the small
things which we take so much for granted in our country.
More serious is the fact that they can rarely afford to buy
books for study, nor do their libraries have resources remotely comparable with those of our institutions. Beyond
this, instruction is frequently anything but inspiring, and
study is constrained and limited because the student is
required by law to pass an annual examination which puts
a high premium on memory work—an examination, set
by an outside examining authority, to which each year
many more are called than can possibly be chosen. And
if a student persists in the face of repeated difficulty and
finally in time earns a degree, there is the further debilitating consideration that his chances of finding an appropriate job are frighteningly slim. Yet so great is his inner
drive and so bright his hope that the Indian student de-
sides education beyond all else, and perseveres.

I had a fear at the time, and do now, that what I said to
the students of Delhi may have seemed strangely unreal
and irrelevant. I spoke to them first of the new interest in
universities that has sprung up all over the world; of how
this is especially noticeable in those countries where
earlier there have been few universities or at any rate few
strong ones. I tried to make them feel some excitement in
this fact. At the same time I endeavored to suggest that the

new interest in universities is neither so firmly based nor
so deeply understanding as it might be. Perhaps this was
gratuitous under the circumstances. I stated that the new
interest in universities, especially in the developing countries, springs from a hunger for the contribution that
universities can make to the solution of such urgent contemporary problems as economic growth, land reform, improved health, efficient administration, better social welfare, labor organization, and even military advantage. I
made the point that in all this there is very little evidence
of concern about learning for learning's sake, and even
less for the joy and the beauty that rightfully make part
of the intellectual process. In many parts of the world
considerations of this kind—which seem to us highly relevant in education—have scarcely had a chance to arise in
the face of an almost exclusive preoccupation with questions of utility.

I spoke also of worries about universities which I have
found to be common among thinking people in all parts
of the world. Is the university a servant of the state?
Should it be? How far can the purposes of a college or a
university be identified with those of a state? Where do
they diverge? Is is possible they can sometimes actually
be in opposition? Are the purposes of a university to be
completely comprehended within the need for technological advance? In this latter matter, has the existence of
material need in underdeveloped parts of the world, con-
joined with the scientific triumphs of the highly developed areas, set loose a force within education which now
threatens to take over the whole enterprise for its own
purpose? And what about the press of numbers and the
problem created for all institutions of higher education,
where the means of institutional growth are so hard to
acquire, by the onrushing tide of population?

These were some of the seemingly universal problems of contemporary education about which I spoke to my new Indian friends.

Morehouse College was founded almost a hundred years ago, before the growth of universities as we now know them in this country. The industrial revolution, gathering strength from science and technology, was then under way; but it would seem that the impetus was less the desire to create and harness institutions of higher learning for national economic development—even for social advance—than to provide citizens with the opportunity for personal development; opportunity to prepare for rewarding jobs, yes, but even more, opportunity to grow as persons. In my view this was good, and I hope we have not outgrown it.

At the same time, in the face of present concerns, the guiding visions of that early period must appear now to have been parochial, limited in geographical awareness, and deficient in social ambition. Nor are the achievements of the early institutions impressive when we measure them by contemporary standards for scholarly research. A hundred years ago the world of higher education was a congeries of little worlds in which the parts had not yet begun to find themselves nor individually to develop the strength they now display. Yet the ideas which guided each of those little worlds continue to impress by virtue of their cheerful hopefulness, their confidence in the power and promise of mind for understanding and personal growth, and even more in their awareness of values and aspirations deeper than those generated simply by immediate economic concern.

The American college was and—in so far as it follows in the path set early for it—continues to be a very special kind of institution. It imparts knowledge, yes, but beyond

this its aim is to bring individuals into a lively awareness
of the conditions and potentials of life; and to strengthen
in them both the desire and the capacity to seek rationally
to direct their lives. It aspires also to make each of us conscious of the best aspects of human achievement and thus
to engender in us an eager desire to play a part in and
align ourselves with kinds of living conducive to these
ends. This it does through its curriculum, but even more
perhaps through its people and its common life.

The early college wished to train the mind and to train
the man. When it said that its purpose was to train the
mind, it meant not so much the addition of something to
a mind but, as a perceptive commentator remarked, doing
something to it. The college's aim was through learning
"to transform the mind at a vital point, the point where its
secret ends reside." It had to be concerned with what a
student knew, but at a deeper level it exercised a pressing
concern for what that student chose finally to do with his
life. And the early college's successor institution, if less
confidently, nevertheless still harbors this ancient, basic
concern.

In Asia today, in Africa, in Latin America, one sees evidence of a driving movement to build more universities.
The governments of the developing nations have a
ravenous hunger for the trained products of universities,
and more and more the young people of these nations are
determined to find a place for themselves in higher education because of the promise it holds for rewarding careers.
Nor is this phenomenon confined to so-called developing
nations. Even in conservative Britain there is a new eagerness to widen educational opportunity and a determination to open halls of learning to the larger fraction of the
population which everyone now recognizes is needed to

perform the skilled services of a growing twentieth-
century industrial society.

India's third five-year plan outlines that country's
strategy for development during the period immediately
ahead. It says that "more than ever before programs of
education lie at the base of the effort to forge the bonds of
common citizenship, to harness the energies of the people
and to develop the natural and human resources of every
part of the country." It states in another part of the docu-
ment that "of all the resources for development perhaps
the most fundamental at the present time is trained manpower." These sentiments are now shared by virtually
every government in the world, if less zealously perhaps
by our own than most others.

At the Delhi commencement, degrees were awarded in
nursing, medicine, agriculture, engineering, business, and
in other subjects for professional training. The gathering
evidenced pride in the achievement of the trainees and joy
in the fact that there were fresh recruits for the ranks of
the ready. Despite some signs of the unspoken fear that
many of these new graduates would not quickly find opportunity for employment even remotely commensurate
with their preparation and ambitions, almost every ges-
ture and word used at this commencement took on its
deeper meaning from an understanding often unspoken
of the relationship which existed between this commencement and the growing national aspiration. A backward
country was stirring to new life. It needed trained young
people to help with the effort. And these the Indian universities in general, and this Indian university in particular, were providing. Here were new recruits ready for the
task. But though this mood was omnipresent, what the
university seemed to be trying most to say to its new

graduates had very little to do with either jobs or development. Its deeper concern was spoken through a little booklet, a copy of which was given to each graduate. This little pamphlet carried two quotations from ancient wisdom literature of India.

One of the quotations bore the title "Advice." The other, longer, one was called "Commandment." The translation accompanying the Hindustani text of the first passage read thus:

Advice

Meet together, talk together:
May your minds comprehend alike
Common be your action and achievement:
Common be your thoughts and intentions:
Common be the wishes of your hearts
—So there may be thorough union among you.

We Americans live in a mature economic society and at first glance seem now to be confronted by few of the practical problems which constrict the lives of even the educated individuals among the masses of India. According to standards applicable over most of the globe, we enjoy what Indians would consider incredible: freedom from hunger, poverty, and disease. One can say this without failing to recognize that we are yet far from having achieved a perfect union here, and this at a time when the concept has taken on an enormously more profound reach than ever before. We know there are many items of unfinished business on our agenda, both for a more acceptable common life at home and for fuller discharge of our growing responsibilities abroad. We continue to have need for people like Ralph Bunche among ourselves and for people like Albert Schweitzer everywhere.

The little passage I have just quoted from the Delhi Commencement booklet suggests what the experience of

attending any good college should have been like. Meet
together, talk together, for the sake of comprehension,
understanding, and union.

Then came the second longer passage in the booklet,
called "Commandment." It read:

Speak the truth;
Practice righteousness;
Do not slacken in your studies;
Give your teacher the honorarium desired by him;
Maintain the continuity of your line;
Never deviate from truth;
Never deviate from rectitude;
Ensure your welfare;
Secure your prosperity;
Cease not to study and teach;
Discharge your duties to the gods and your ancestors;
Adore your mother as a god;
Adore your father as a god;
Respect your teacher as a god;
Honor your guest as a god;
Do only irreproachable acts, not others;
Follow only our right courses of conduct, not others;
Honor your betters with a seat, when they go to you;
Make gift with respect;
Don't give disrespectfully;
Give with grace;
Give with modesty;
Give with humility;
Give with understanding sympathy;
If you should still have doubt concerning your course of action
    or concerning your conduct in a given situation, deport
    yourself in the same manner as men who are competent to
    judge, devoted, gentle and prone to righteousness, would do
    in such a situation.
With regard to men of doubtful character, behave yourselves
    as men with the aforesaid qualities would behave with re-
    gard to such men;
This is the precept;

This is the advice;
This is the path and substance of all Scriptural teaching;
This is the commandment;
Follow it; follow it.

There is much in this that seems strange to us—parts of it perhaps definitely out of place. Yet it was this, rather than any modern exhortation to industrial efficiency, which represented Delhi University's concluding word to her graduates. There is no mention of industry, technology, development, or administration. Nothing of national pride nor of world prestige. Rather essentially only an instruction to an individual person to speak the truth and to practice righteousness.

Is not this essentially what college seeks to say to all of us?

In an age of claims and counterclaims, of deliberate misrepresentations and all kinds of strident nonsense; at a time when, at first glance, many people and even whole nations seem to be animated by a ruthless ambition to get on and get up, such words win few hearers. Today governments impatiently want from universities trained people with drive and energy. They need them, and the universities seek to provide them, but in the very midst of this task, in a moment of special seriousness one university, set among great adversities, wished to turn back to say to its sons and daughters not simply "Build and prosper" but much more, "Speak the truth and practice righteousness."

This is an ancient lesson in colleges and universities. The twofold injunction provides the basic aim of our directing purpose; the tradition of learning has never quite eschewed its moral component: not truth only, but truth and righteousness. Today, beset more severely than ever before by pressing practical considerations, we per-

haps too easily overlook this. Needs, numbers, impatience
to get on in such a time—it was interesting to me and I
hope it will be to you that halfway round the world the
University of Delhi, oppressed by practical concerns as
few universities in our country can be, chose to speak to
its graduates at the end of their university careers not of
the problems of industrialization and the strategy of development, but rather of ancient moral concerns.

The University of Delhi, though larger now, is not so
old as Morehouse College. Morehouse, Harvard, and all
of ours belong with Delhi and other colleges and universities, new and old, everywhere, in one common tradition.
We are all members of an ancient fellowship of educated
men and women whose numbers though relatively small
and whose voices though relatively feeble are, I am convinced, the best hope of mankind. It is a thin and fragile
chain that binds Morehouse and Harvard with Delhi and
a thousand other institutions where learning flourishes
and is honored, and where the noblest qualities of man
stand revealed in that simple and unpretentious Indian
"commandment": truth and righteousness, and with them
courage, modesty, sympathy, belief, understanding, and
joy.

At any commencement there is little more we can say
than what they said:

> This is the precept;
> This is the advice;
> This is the commandment;
> Follow it; follow it.

In the widespread observance of such commandment,
under God, lies our hope for a better world.

* * * * * * *

KNOWLEDGE, FAITH, AND THE QUALITY OF LIFE

Last november in an Indian newspaper there appeared an editorial with the title "A Nation of Slovens." The phrase originated with Prime Minister Nehru, who had applied it to his fellow countrymen in an address delivered a day or two previously to the chancellors of India's more than forty universities.

The issue which had provoked this name-calling did not seem to me very important. It was a question as to whether or not Indian school children should wear uniforms, as French children do, and Japanese. Mr. Nehru felt they should. Apparently others had disagreed. In making his case Mr. Nehru had said, "We are, by and large—not everybody—a slovenly people."

I was startled by the statement, since it is not the kind of remark we would expect a political leader to make about his compatriots, especially when an election is coming up. I was even more surprised at the obvious relish with which the writer of the editorial, presumably Indian, picked up the remark and developed it. "The untidy Indian," he wrote, "is ubiquitous. He dresses in a thousand different ways, and all of them sloppy. He eats messily . . . as if the few moments he would have to spend gracefully eating his meal would be an unpardonable waste of

Baccalaureate Sermon for the senior class of Harvard College, Harvard Memorial Church, June 10, 1962.

time. His health and hygiene habits are not the most imitable or worthy of admiration or publicity; he would think nothing of picking his nose in a bus, or clearing his throat with a maximum of noise, or even disposing of the remains of the well-chewed *pan* (betel leaf) in a far from restrained manner. He is a stranger to discipline, viewing the disciplinarians with disfavor and as cranky intruders into what he considers his private and exclusive domain. His norms of social behavior are appallingly poor. And what is more, the slovenly Indian is clumsy and unmethodical in his very thinking and speaking. Much might be forgiven him; but slovenly thinking will in the long run spell his ruin."

I was in no position to tell whether this represented honest criticism or abuse, and I still am not; but before I left India I had developed considerable sympathy for Nehru because of the magnitude of the difficulties with which he is confronted as the leader of a great country poorly prepared for the new kind of existence it is now endeavoring to lead. If there is an issue here and one has to choose between Nehru and his people my initial sympathy would be with him. But there is much to be said on the other side.

The writer of the editorial undertook at once to redress the balance. "Of course," he went on to say, "there are 'reasons' for all this depressing state of affairs. By and large he (that is today's Indian) is still a victim of grinding poverty; greed, ignorance, isolationism, diffidence, and a pervasive sense of insecurity contribute to the untidiness and frustration of his thinking and behavior. He has come to put up with his lot with an incredible amount of resignation and fatalism, and the very urges that should make him go and break his chains are lost in the welter of his own private affairs and thoughts; he is too engrossed in them to realize that there are others about him; his eye is cast inward and he has absolutely no consideration for others."

Political leaders in the United States usually confine their attacks to their counterparts in the other party. They are not accustomed to making deprecatory remarks about us, their fellow citizens; certainly not to large numbers of us at any one time, for we might not elect them if they did. But though they may fail us in respect to candor, we do not lack for critics. Other individuals eager to point out our faults spring up everywhere. Recently, for example, we were categorized as "a nation of sheep." The author of the book with this title had collaborated earlier in the writing of another successful publication called *The Ugly American*. Neither of these books, as the titles suggest, was intended to paint a very flattering portrait of us. And they are not the only examples of their kind.

The books just mentioned grew out of their authors' experience abroad, especially in Asia. We cannot quarrel with the view that one of the purposes of traveling abroad is to try to find out what other people are like, and another is to learn from them; even, hopefully, to learn something about ourselves. But there is an aspect in which this latter can be overdone, for it is easy to be so concerned about what others think of us that we become, as a people, as debilitatingly self-conscious as are some individuals. We are all too familiar with those who in an instance of national difficulty immediately conclude that our position is wholly attributable to our own stupidity; that we are embarrassed because we did something we should not have done, or because we failed to do something we should have done; that circumstances had very little to do with it; and that once again our opponents have shown themselves to be infinitely more perceptive, imaginative, and understanding than we. Many Americans have the unhappy proclivity of seeing virtue in others at their own expense, just as in an earlier generation there were too many Americans who assumed that anything foreign was wrong. But it seems to me patent nonsense to assume that the world's ills are invariably due to American ignorance and greed. A hard, honest look almost anywhere today will quickly dispel the notion that all the world's blindness, selfishness, and malice are lodged with us.

People in Asia are impressed by America's might and wealth. They recognize that our country has become one of the world's very great powers—perhaps, *the* great power. They have learned that our power owes much to the enormous industrial and economic development which occurred here during the past century and a half and which still goes on. They have come to understand that this kind of development is nourished by education, science, and technology. They are willing to acknowledge that it may owe something to political freedom. They respect, even admire, our achievement, at least in part, and now eagerly want something like it for themselves. They wish to escape from the misery and the drudgery characteristic of life in ancient countries which have the capital and technology to support only a mean and precarious existence by painful age-old, inadequate routines. They passionately desire the plenty, education, and health, and the chance for the fuller life, which the machine has given to the West. From this point of view, therefore, we can say that they admire us; and it is perhaps not too much to add that they actually envy us. But at the same time, looking at us and at other Western nations, the perceptive among them are terrified by a fear of what a development similar to ours might do to them. Adequate food, greater comfort, cleanliness, jobs and employment, some recreation and leisure—these things of course they want. But other things which they discern in our society they clearly do not want, and if these latter are inevitable concomitants, they are not at all sure they wish to pay the price.

It is important for us to know that not all observers of America in underdeveloped countries accept at face value what we present as a true picture of ourselves—a nation of energetic, independent, happy, free men, intelligently and modestly enjoying one of the highest standards of living ever achieved on this globe. Looking behind our huckster advertising, our self-serving political speeches, and our slick-paper accounts of ourselves, they discern, not a nation of happy people living responsibly in a society permeated with justice and mercy, but a national life marred by much frustration and emptiness, hardness and indifference, loneliness and insecurity, selfishness; and, along with such personal characteristics, fragmented relationships, broken homes, drunkenness, juvenile delinquency, race prejudice, snobbery of class, irresponsibility, and a host of other evidences of emotional ill health which we minimize, overlook, or pretend to ignore. These critical observers see in us, the operators of a modern industrial nation, not slovens, certainly, nor even sheep, but a variety of self-seeking thoughtless, unattractive people, careless of decency, eager to impress; and they are quite sure—the thoughtful among them—that they do not want to be recreated in our image, not even at the cost of the plenty and the health they so passionately desire and so patently need. Something like this, I take it, was a substratum of Gandhi's view; and in it is posed for us a question.

The old Greek concept of the *oikumene,* the inhabited world, is now being stretched until it begins in fact to en-

compass the whole of the planet, as peoples everywhere
come inescapably to live in awareness and in involvement
with each other. If we stand back and look at the
oikumene, what we see is that a revolution which began in
the West some generations past has now called us in America to leadership, whether we like it or not, as it advances
over the whole world. We here should all pray, I feel, for
its accelerated progress; for surely poverty, want, ignorance, and ill health are not things to be treasured anywhere on the earth. But at the same time we must be
aware of the thought of those like the Indians, waiting
expectantly and at the same time apprehensively. To their
leader, impatient to move forward, the unindustrialized
Indian may seem a sloven. So too, to others, incidentally,
may have seemed our ancestors in an unwashed England
and more recently closer to home. It may also be that the
Indian could be doing much more for himself than he is.
But surely Asian slovenliness, real or imputed, of however
great concern to Mr. Nehru, is not now for the world the
basic concern. Is it not rather the spiritual capacity—or
lack of it—in Occidental, industrial man?

To many in the underdeveloped parts of the world we
in the West, especially we Americans, seem to be shallow,
arrogant, almost exclusively preoccupied with material-
istic pursuits. We know this caricature does not represent
the full truth about us. We should like to think that it
may even be libelous. But at the same time we have a
haunting doubt that it may not be completely wide of the
mark. What kind of people are we really?

There is of course no simple answer to this, for we are
all kinds and no kind, just as other peoples are—good,
bad, and indifferent. Mr. Nehru compained before a
group of vice-chancellors that his people were deficient in
industry, were generally sloppy—that they lacked order

and discipline. What would a similarly perceptive and honest leader in a comparable position here say of us? I do not know, but I raise the question, since in my view it is in places like this, among groups like ourselves who have had advantages—perhaps especially on occasions like this when we should feel some sense of participation in a numerous, dedicated, enduring community—that the question ought to be raised. And it is a question to which we should have an answer.

Americans are not inferior to or more self-seeking than other peoples. On the whole I should be prepared to defend the thesis that they are rather better, in the sense of being more truly concerned for others, than are most. Nor is our present position of power in the world—assuming it is a good thing for us—wholly due to luck. We need not waste time in apologies. But we must be constantly concerned for the quality of our life, and increasingly now, as this manner of life is exerting an influence—making converts or repelling—all over the world.

The writer of the editorial to which I have referred argued that a greater sense of discipline would have to be inculcated in India. "By a process of teaching and propaganda," he said, today's Indian "should be made alive to his civic duties. He should be made to learn that without discipline life has no meaning whatever. Some of the remedies cannot wait until the slovenly man completes his self-education; they have to be imposed on him—with the minimum necessary pressure but with some pressure recognizable as such. Some people might protest; but they will soon realize that this is the quickest way to knock the slovenliness out of him."

One can have considerable sympathy with the writer's and Mr. Nehru's impatience, and some among us might agree that this is a good way to proceed, as surely most of our Puritan ancestors would have done. But, in our present majority view, discipline and civic duty are not things which can be driven into a person from the outside. There are generations of ineffective efforts to prove this point. In our view such qualities must be self-developed if they are to be had; or perhaps we should say rather, such qualities can and may grow in a person in a favorable environment if the heart is set upon them.

What then of the heart? More specifically, what has been the effect of the experience of Harvard, if any, on the hearts of her sons?

For a long time college faculties out of a modest sense of futility and incompetence have tended to disclaim any interest in a responsibility for what used to be called moral education. Even college presidents have long since given over their early practice of offering formal instruction in the subject. Indeed it is possible now to make a case that there has been widespread defection from liberal education, in so far as this phrase denotes a program of instruction which seeks deliberately to effect changes—perhaps even improvements—in the desiring parts of our natures by endeavoring to draw us through deepened intellectual experience into full humanity. Today we are not wanting experts of a sort who tell us that virtually the whole enterprise of higher education in this country, when it is measured by its ability to produce fundamental changes in the natures of those who have experienced it, is a failure. To impart information, to build experience—yes, perhaps; but to develop concerned citizens and devoted leaders—nonsense, this it does not and cannot do.

And yet I wonder.

Year after year recently the annual reports of the graduate secretaries of the Phillips Brooks House have carried impressive statistics of participation by undergraduates in the House's many and varied welfare programs. Some six hundred students of Harvard and Radcliffe participated in these affairs this year and last. Months before the Peace Corps got under way last year, a group of students here somewhere found the initiative and energy, and demonstrated the concern and the ability, to organize and carry out Project Tanganyika.* The performance of the recent Combined Charities Drives has been impressive and heartening. Scarcely anything could have been more exciting than the way the Glee Club, always ready to sing at all college occasions, conceived, planned, and carried out its expedition to East Asia; or the somewhat similar plan of the Orchestra to carry out a mission of music at a high professional level to Mexico. All this while more than half the upperclassmen have been busy working for degrees with honors. And there has been much other meritorious activity in drama, athletics, art, debating, politics, and new publishing ventures. Surely the individuals who achieved this full record were not unconcerned persons, lost—as today's Indians are said by Nehru to be and today's Americans by others—"in the welter of their own private affairs and thoughts." Rather, it seems to me indisputable that these are the achievements of men of ability who both care and do.

What Harvard wants more than anything now to give to our country and the world is educated men—and women —of character. It is her hope that there will develop here generation after generation, now as in the past, thoughtful

* "Operation Tanganyika" has been a project of the Phillips Brooks House Association, undergraduate interreligious social service organization at Harvard. Beginning in 1961, the Program has annually arranged to send sixteen to twenty students to Tanganyika for periods of three or fifteen months. The students serve as teachers of English and supervisors of recreational programs at Dar es Salaam. The Association also sponsors a Brooks House course in Swahili and various African subjects and helps stimulate African student exchanges to this country.

men who through their beliefs and actions will go on to renew and strengthen true quality in the world's life; men and women of knowledge and faith who, ready to learn from others, will make an effort at honest appraisal of their culture, will recognize both its strength and its weakness, will try to see these aspects separately and fairly, and who then, not complaining, or criticizing unreasonably, or turning away in supercilious indifference, will steadfastly set about working where they can—first of all perhaps with themselves—to improve that culture and to make not its shabbiness but its goodness available to others.

These last four years have seen a multiplication of tension in the world. Three billion people, most of them moving from the land into cities, all but a few hundred million of them virtually destitute; and the number will probably have doubled in the next generation. What can one life be—what can it mean among so many? No one can say, but each of us has a life to live, and we shall want to spend it as well as may be—neither as slovens nor as sheep, but as alert, fair, concerned citizens of a complicated human world, aware in some fashion of God's high purpose for this earth of ours, eager to have a part in His plan for it, and to find joy in the process!

* * * * * * *

REFERENCES

A FAITH FOR THESE TIMES

The text of "The Religion of the Future" may be found in Charles W. Eliot, *The Durable Satisfactions of Life* (New York: T. Y. Crowell Company, 1910), or in *Charles W. Eliot, The Man and His Beliefs*, edited with a biographical study by William Allan Neilson (New York and London: Harper & Brothers, 1926), II, 576–603.

FREEDOM, LOYALTY, AND THE AMERICAN UNIVERSITY

A very interesting discussion of the history of the institutional freedom in the German universities is contained in Edward Yarnell Hartshorne, *German Universities and National Socialism* (Cambridge, Massachusetts: Harvard University Press, 1937), pp. 40–71. The translation of Bernhard's statement is also by Hartshorne, pp. 45–56, taken from Bernhard, *Academische Selbstsverwaltung in Frankreich und Deutschland* (Berlin, 1930). For a general reference work on the question, see Friedrich Paulsen, *Geschichte des gelehrten Unterrichts* . . . 2 vols. (Leipzig, 1919–21), and his volume *The German Universities, Their Character and Historical Development*, authorized translation by Edward Delavan Perry (New York: Macmillan, 1895).

The quotation from President Eliot is taken from Mr. Eliot's inaugural address, October 19, 1869. See Neilson, *Charles William Eliot*, I, 21.

EDUCATION FOR FREE MEN

Samuel Eliot Morison in *The Founding of Harvard College* (Cambridge, Massachusetts: Harvard University Press, 1935), p. 157, states that the vote of the Town of Boston regarding Mr. Pormort, April 13, 1635, is the beginning of the recorded history of New England schools.

LEADERSHIP AND THE AMERICAN UNIVERSITY

George H. Williams' account of the theology and religious sources of the idea of a university appears in Sydney E. Ahlstrom and others, *The Harvard Divinity School: Its Place in Harvard University and in American Culture* (Boston: The Beacon Press, 1954), pp. 230–248 and 295–351. The reader may also wish to refer to Robert Ulich, *The Human Career, A Philosophy of Self-Transcendence* (New York: Harper & Brothers, 1955).

Richard Hofstadter's essay "The Development of Higher Education in America" appears in Richard Hofstadter and C. DeWitt Hardy, *The Development and Scope of Higher Education* (New York: Columbia University Press, 1952). The greatly abbreviated statement on pp. 50–51 comes from Henry Wriston, *The Nature of the Liberal Arts College* (Appleton, Wisconsin: Lawrence College Press, 1937).

JUSTICE, THE UNIVERSITY, AND THE PROFESSIONS

The mention of the hawk and the nightingale and of the "crooked judgments" of "gift devouring princes" refers to a famous passage in Hesiod's *Works and Days*. See the Loeb Classical Library edition, pp. 19–23.

Plato's account of the conversation between Socrates and the aged Cephalus on the nature of justice occurs in the first book of *The Republic*.

Mr. Justice Jackson's Godkin Lectures were posthumously published; see Robert H. Jackson, *The Supreme Court in the American System of Government* (Cambridge, Massachusetts: Harvard University Press, 1955).

The late Sir Thomas M. Taylor, Principal of the University of Aberdeen, is the source of the apt quotation about "a long look in the dark."

Two works mentioned which helped to throw light on the question of communism and civil liberties in the United States are *Digest of the Public Record of Communism in the United States,* edited by Charles Corker, Clinton P. Rossiter, Joseph M. Snee, S.J., and Arthur E. Sutherland (Cambridge, Massachusetts, published for the Fund for the Republic, Inc., 1955), and Samuel A. Stouffer, *Communism, Conformity, and Civil Liberties; A Cross-Section of the Nation Speaks Its Mind* (Garden City: Doubleday & Company, 1955).

COLONEL WILLIAMS' LEGACY

Carroll Perry in *A Professor of Life* (Boston: Houghton Mifflin Company, 1923) gives a delightful picture of his father, Professor Arthur Latham Perry, and, through his father's writings, of President Hopkins and the Williams College of the mid-nineteenth century.

Mark Hopkins' life has been chronicled by two different biographers: Franklin Carter, *Mark Hopkins* (Boston: Houghton Mifflin, 1892), and John Hopkins Denison, *Mark Hopkins: A Biography* (New York: Charles Scribner's Sons, 1935).

EDUCATION AND MEDICINE

Henry James, *Charles W. Eliot* (Boston: Houghton Mifflin Company, 1930), pp. 273–293, contains a good general account of Mr. Eliot's struggles to bring the Medical School more truly into the university framework and reform its program. A more academic account is that of Frederick C. Shattuck and J. Lewis Bremer, "The Medical School 1869–1929," in Samuel Eliot Morison, *Development of Harvard University since the Inauguration of President Eliot* (Cambridge, Massachusetts: Harvard University Press, 1930).

The phrase from William Temple (1881–1944), Archbishop of Canterbury, comes from "Freedom, Peace and Truth," a sermon preached before the University of Oxford, and is quoted in Walter Moberly, *The Crisis in the University* (London: S.C.M. Press Ltd., 1949), pp. 58–59. Temple is credited with having "stopped the rot" in the Christian life of Oxford following the First World War. His "missions" to Oxford, Cambridge, London, Leeds, and Newcastle made a deep impression on the students.

AN ISLAND OF LIGHT

John Livingston Lowes was Professor of English at Harvard from 1918 to 1930 and Francis Lee Higginson Professor of English Literature from 1930 to 1939. He was the author of *The Road to Xanadu* (1927). Irving Babbitt was a teacher at Harvard for nearly forty years and served as Professor of French Literature from 1912 until his death in 1933. He wrote *Rousseau and Romanticism* (1919).

THE AGE OF THE SCHOLAR

For the story of the founding of Johns Hopkins and the long friendship between Mr. Eliot and Mr. Gilman, see Fabian Franklin, *The Life of Daniel Coit Gilman* (New York: Dodd Mead and Company, 1910) and Henry James, *Charles W. Eliot*, cited above.

SECULARISM AND THE JOY OF BELIEF

The allusions here are to Walter Moberly, *The Crisis in the University*, p. 55, and to J. H. Oldham, *Life is Commitment* (New York: Harper & Brothers, 1952), p. 25 and p. 58.

UTILITY AND THE AMERICAN UNIVERSITY

The anecdote about Andrew Dickson White comes from the *Autobiography of Andrew Dickson White* (New York: The Century Company, 1905), I, 303.

THE JOINT RESPONSIBILITY OF PUBLIC
AND PRIVATE UNIVERSITIES

For an account of the early development of colleges and universities in the United States, see George P. Schmidt, *The Old Time College President* (New York: Columbia University Press, 1930), Donald G. Tewksbury, *The Founding of American Colleges and Universities Before the Civil War* (New York: Teachers College, Columbia University, 1932), and Richard Hofstadter and Walter P. Metzger, *The Development of Academic Freedom in the United States* (New York: Columbia University Press, 1955). The allusion to the discussion of the Jeffersonian and Jacksonian emphasis in American education is in *General Education in a Free Society, Report of the Harvard Committee* (Cambridge, Massachusetts: Harvard University Press, 1945).

COLLEGE EDUCATION AND MORAL CHARACTER

An entertaining history of the early leaders of American colleges and their views of the scope of moral education is contained in George P. Schmidt, *The Old Time College President,* cited above.

Dean Horton's Beecher Lectures have been published in Douglas Horton, *The Meaning of Worship,* The Lyman Beecher Lectures for 1958 (New York: Harper & Brothers, 1959).

THE AMERICAN UNIVERSITY 1960

The quotations from Paulsen and Savigny are taken from Friedrich Paulsen, *The German Universities, Their Character and Historical Development,* pp. 236–238.

Revised November, 1964

harper ⚜ torchbooks

HUMANITIES AND SOCIAL SCIENCES

American Studies

JOHN R. ALDEN: The American Revolution, 1775-1783.† Illus.　　　　　TB/3011

BERNARD BAILYN: The New England Merchants in the Seventeenth Century　　TB/1149

RAY STANNARD BAKER: Following the Color Line: American Negro Citizenship in the Progressive Era.‡ Illus. Edited by Dewey W. Grantham, Jr.　TB/3053

RAY A. BILLINGTON: The Far Western Frontier, 1830-1860.† Illus.　　　　TB/3012

JOSEPH L. BLAU, Ed.: Cornerstones of Religious Freedom in America. Selected Basic Documents, Court Decisions and Public Statements. Revised and Enlarged Edition　　　　　　TB/118

RANDOLPH S. BOURNE: War and the Intellectuals: Collected Essays, 1915-1919.‡ Edited by Carl Resek　　　　　　TB/3043

A. RUSSELL BUCHANAN: The United States and World War II. † Illus.　　Vol. I TB/3044
　　　　　　　　　　　　　　Vol. II TB/3045

ABRAHAM CAHAN: The Rise of David Levinsky: a novel. Introduction by John Higham　TB/1028

JOSEPH CHARLES: The Origins of the American Party System　　　　　　TB/1049

THOMAS C. COCHRAN: The Inner Revolution: Essays on the Social Sciences in History　TB/1140

T. C. COCHRAN & WILLIAM MILLER: The Age of Enterprise: A Social History of Industrial America　　　　　　TB/1054

EDWARD S. CORWIN: American Constitutional History: Essays edited by Alpheus T. Mason and Gerald Garvey　　　　　　TB/1136

FOSTER RHEA DULLES: America's Rise to World Power, 1898-1954.† Illus.　TB/3021

W. A. DUNNING: Reconstruction, Political and Economic, 1865-1877　　TB/1073

A. HUNTER DUPREE: Science in the Federal Government: A History of Policies and Activities to 1940　　　　　　TB/573

CLEMENT EATON: The Freedom-of-Thought Struggle in the Old South. Revised Edition. Illus. TB/1150

CLEMENT EATON: The Growth of Southern Civilization, 1790-1860.† Illus.　TB/3040

HAROLD U. FAULKNER: Politics, Reform and Expansion, 1890-1900.† Illus.　TB/3020

LOUIS FILLER: The Crusade against Slavery, 1830-1860.† Illus.　　　　TB/3029

EDITORS OF FORTUNE: America in the Sixties: the Economy and the Society. 72 two-color charts　　　　　　TB/1015

DIXON RYAN FOX: The Decline of Aristocracy in the Politics of New York.‡ Edited by Robert V. Remini　　　　　　TB/3064

LAWRENCE HENRY GIPSON: The Coming of the Revolution, 1763-1775.† Illus.　TB/3007

FRANCIS J. GRUND: Aristocracy in America: Jacksonian Democracy　　　TB/1001

ALEXANDER HAMILTON: The Reports of Alexander Hamilton.‡ Edited by Jacob E. Cooke　TB/3060

OSCAR HANDLIN, Editor: This Was America: As Recorded by European Travelers to the Western Shore in the Eighteenth, Nineteenth, and Twentieth Centuries. Illus.　　　　　TB/1119

MARCUS LEE HANSEN: The Atlantic Migration: 1607-1860. Edited by Arthur M. Schlesinger, Sr.; Introduction by Oscar Handlin　　TB/1052

MARCUS LEE HANSEN: The Immigrant in American History. Edited with a Foreword by Arthur M. Schlesinger, Sr.　　　　TB/1120

JOHN D. HICKS: Republican Ascendancy, 1921-1933.† Illus.　　　　TB/3041

JOHN HIGHAM, Ed.: The Reconstruction of American History　　　　　TB/1068

† The New American Nation Series, edited by Henry Steele Commager and Richard B. Morris.
‡ American Perspectives series, edited by Bernard Wishy and William E. Leuchtenburg.
* The Rise of Modern Europe series, edited by William L. Langer.
‖ Researches in the Social, Cultural, and Behavioral Sciences, edited by Benjamin Nelson.
§ The Library of Religion and Culture, edited by Benjamin Nelson.
Σ Harper Modern Science Series, edited by James R. Newman.
° Not for sale in Canada.

Anthropology & Sociology

PITIRIM SOROKIN: Contemporary Sociological Theories. *Through the First Quarter of the Twentieth Century* TB/3046

MAURICE R. STEIN: The Eclipse of Community: *An Interpretation of American Studies.* TB/1128

SIR EDWARD TYLOR: The Origins of Culture. *Part I of "Primitive Culture."§ Introduction by Paul Radin* TB/33

SIR EDWARD TYLOR: Religion in Primitive Culture. *Part II of "Primitive Culture."§ Introduction by Paul Radin* TB/34

W. LLOYD WARNER & Associates: Democracy in Jonesville: *A Study in Quality and Inequality* TB/1129

W. LLOYD WARNER: A Black Civilization: *A Study of an Australian Tribe.* Illus. TB/3056

W. LLOYD WARNER: Social Class in America: *The Evaluation of Status* TB/1013

Art and Art History

WALTER LOWRIE: Art in the Early Church. *Illus. Revised Edition* TB/124

EMILE MÂLE: The Gothic Image: *Religious Art in France of the Thirteenth Century.§ 190 illus.* TB/44

MILLARD MEISS: Painting in Florence and Siena after the Black Death: *The Arts, Religion and Society in the Mid-Fourteenth Century. 169 illus.* TB/1148

ERICH NEUMANN: The Archetypal World of Henry Moore. *107 illus.* TB/2020

ERWIN PANOFSKY: Studies in Iconology: *Humanistic Themes in the Art of the Renaissance. 180 illustrations* TB/1077

ALEXANDRE PIANKOFF: The Shrines of Tut-Ankh-Amon. *Edited by N. Rambova. 117 illus.* TB/2011

JEAN SEZNEC: The Survival of the Pagan Gods: *The Mythological Tradition and Its Place in Renaissance Humanism and Art. 108 illustrations* TB/2004

OTTO VON SIMSON: The Gothic Cathedral: *Origins of Gothic Architecture and the Medieval Concept of Order. 58 illus.* TB/2018

HEINRICH ZIMMER: Myths and Symbols in Indian Art and Civilization. *70 illustrations* TB/2005

Business, Economics & Economic History

REINHARD BENDIX: Work and Authority in Industry: *Ideologies of Management in the Course of Industrialization* TB/3035

THOMAS C. COCHRAN: The American Business System: *A Historical Perspective, 1900-1955* TB/1080

ROBERT DAHL & CHARLES E. LINDBLOM: Politics, Economics, and Welfare: *Planning and Politico-Economic Systems Resolved into Basic Social Processes* TB/3037

PETER F. DRUCKER: The New Society: *The Anatomy of Industrial Order* TB/1082

ROBERT L. HEILBRONER: The Great Ascent: *The Struggle for Economic Development in Our Time* TB/3030

ABBA P. LERNER: Everybody's Business: *Current Assumptions in Economics and Public Policy* TB/3051

ROBERT GREEN McCLOSKEY: American Conservatism in the Age of Enterprise, 1865-1910 TB/1137

PAUL MANTOUX: The Industrial Revolution in the Eighteenth Century: *The Beginnings of the Modern Factory System in England* ° TB/1079

WILLIAM MILLER, Ed.: Men in Business: *Essays on the Historical Role of the Entrepreneur* TB/1081

PERRIN STRYKER: The Character of the Executive: *Eleven Studies in Managerial Qualities* TB/1041

PIERRE URI: Partnership for Progress: *A Program for Transatlantic Action* TB/3036

Contemporary Culture

JACQUES BARZUN: The House of Intellect TB/1051

JOHN U. NEF: Cultural Foundations of Industrial Civilization TB/1024

NATHAN M. PUSEY: The Age of the Scholar: *Observations on Education in a Troubled Decade* TB/1157

PAUL VALÉRY: The Outlook for Intelligence TB/2016

History: General

L. CARRINGTON GOODRICH: A Short History of the Chinese People. *Illus.* TB/3015

BERNARD LEWIS: The Arabs in History TB/1029

SIR PERCY SYKES: A History of Exploration.° *Introduction by John K. Wright* TB/1046

History: Ancient and Medieval

A. ANDREWES: The Greek Tyrants TB/1103

P. BOISSONNADE: Life and Work in Medieval Europe: *The Evolution of the Medieval Economy, the Fifth to the Fifteenth Centuries.° Preface by Lynn White, Jr.* TB/1141

HELEN CAM: England before Elizabeth TB/1026

G. G. COULTON: Medieval Village, Manor, and Monastery TB/1022

HEINRICH FICHTENAU: The Carolingian Empire: *The Age of Charlemagne* TB/1142

F. L. GANSHOF: Feudalism TB/1058

J. M. HUSSEY: The Byzantine World TB/1057

SAMUEL NOAH KRAMER: Sumerian Mythology TB/1055

FERDINAND LOT: The End of the Ancient World and the Beginnings of the Middle Ages. *Introduction by Glanville Downey* TB/1044

CHARLES PETIT-DUTAILLIS: The Feudal Monarchy in France and England: *From the Tenth to the Thirteenth Century* ° TB/1165

STEVEN RUNCIMAN: A History of the Crusades. *Volume I: The First Crusade and the Foundation of the Kingdom of Jerusalem. Illus.* TB/1143

FERDINAND SCHEVILL: Siena: *The History of a Medieval Commune. Introduction by William M. Bowsky* TB/1164

HENRY OSBORN TAYLOR: The Classical Heritage of the Middle Ages. *Foreword and Biblio. by Kenneth M. Setton [Formerly listed as TB/48 under the title The Emergence of Christian Culture in the West]* TB/1117

J. M. WALLACE-HADRILL: The Barbarian West: *The Early Middle Ages, A.D. 400-1000* TB/1061

3

History: Renaissance & Reformation

R. R. BOLGAR: The Classical Heritage and Its Beneficiaries: *From the Carolingian Age to the End of the Renaissance*　　　TB/1125

JACOB BURCKHARDT: The Civilization of the Renaissance in Italy. *Introduction by Benjamin Nelson and Charles Trinkaus. Illus.*　　　Volume I TB/40
　　　　　　　　　　　　　　Volume II TB/41

ERNST CASSIRER: The Individual and the Cosmos in Renaissance Philosophy. *Translated with an Introduction by Mario Domandi*　　　TB/1097

EDWARD P. CHEYNEY: The Dawn of a New Era, 1250-1453.* *Illus.*　　　TB/3002

DESIDERIUS ERASMUS: Christian Humanism and the Reformation: *Selected Writings. Edited and translated by John C. Olin*　　　TB/1166

WALLACE K. FERGUSON et al.: Facets of the Renaissance　　　TB/1098

WALLACE K. FERGUSON et al.: The Renaissance: *Six Essays. Illus.*　　　TB/1084

MYRON P. GILMORE: The World of Humanism, 1453-1517.* *Illus.*　　　TB/3003

FRANCESCO GUICCIARDINI: Maxims and Reflections of a Renaissance Statesman: *Ricordi. Trans. by Mario Domandi. Intro. by Nicolai Rubinstein*　　　TB/1160

JOHAN HUIZINGA: Erasmus and the Age of Reformation. *Illus.*　　　TB/19

ULRICH VON HUTTEN et al.: On the Eve of the Reformation: *"Letters of Obscure Men." Introduction by Hajo Holborn*　　　TB/1124

PAUL O. KRISTELLER: Renaissance Thought: *The Classic, Scholastic, and Humanist Strains*　　TB/1048

PAUL O. KRISTELLER: Renaissance Thought II: *Papers on Humanism and the Arts*　　　TB/1163

NICCOLÒ MACHIAVELLI: History of Florence and of the Affairs of Italy: *from the earliest times to the death of Lorenzo the Magnificent. Introduction by Felix Gilbert*　　　TB/1027

ALFRED VON MARTIN: Sociology of the Renaissance. *Introduction by Wallace K. Ferguson*　　　TB/1099

GARRETT MATTINGLY et al.: Renaissance Profiles. *Edited by J. H. Plumb*　　　TB/1162

MILLARD MEISS: Painting in Florence and Siena after the Black Death. *The Arts, Religion and Society in the Mid-Fourteenth Century. 169 illus.*　　TB/1148

J. E. NEALE: The Age of Catherine de Medici[o]　　　TB/1085

ERWIN PANOFSKY: Studies in Iconology: *Humanistic Themes in the Art of the Renaissance. 180 illustrations*　　　TB/1077

J. H. PARRY: The Establishment of the European Hegemony: 1415-1715　　　TB/1045

HENRI PIRENNE: Early Democracies in the Low Countries: *Urban Society and Political Conflict in the Middle Ages and the Renaissance. Introduction by John Mundy*　　　TB/1110

J. H. PLUMB: The Italian Renaissance: *A Concise Survey of Its History and Culture*　　　TB/1161

FERDINAND SCHEVILL: The Medici. *Illus.*　　TB/1010

FERDINAND SCHEVILL: Medieval and Renaissance Florence. *Illus.* Volume I: *Medieval Florence*　　TB/1090
　　　　　Volume II: *The Coming of Humanism and the Age of the Medici*　　　TB/1091

G. M. TREVELYAN: England in the Age of Wycliffe, 1368-1520[o]　　　TB/1112

VESPASIANO: Renaissance Princes, Popes, and Prelates: *The Vespasiano Memoirs: Lives of Illustrious Men of the XVth Century. Introduction by Myron P. Gilmore*　　　TB/1111

History: Modern European

FREDERICK B. ARTZ: Reaction and Revolution, 1815-1832.* *Illus.*　　　TB/3034

MAX BELOFF: The Age of Absolutism, 1660-1815　　　TB/1062

ROBERT C. BINKLEY: Realism and Nationalism, 1852-1871.* *Illus.*　　　TB/3038

CRANE BRINTON: A Decade of Revolution, 1789-1799.* *Illus.*　　　TB/3018

J. BRONOWSKI & BRUCE MAZLISH: The Western Intellectual Tradition: *From Leonardo to Hegel*　　　TB/3001

GEOFFREY BRUUN: Europe and the French Imperium, 1799-1814.* *Illus.*　　　TB/3033

ALAN BULLOCK: Hitler, A Study in Tyranny.[o] *Illus.*　　　TB/1123

E. H. CARR: The Twenty Years' Crisis, 1919-1939: *An Introduction to the Study of International Relations[o]*　　　TB/1122

GORDON A. CRAIG: From Bismarck to Adenauer: *Aspects of German Statecraft. Revised Edition*　　　TB/1171

WALTER L. DORN: Competition for Empire, 1740-1763.* *Illus.*　　　TB/3032

CARL J. FRIEDRICH: The Age of the Baroque, 1610-1660.* *Illus.*　　　TB/3004

LEO GERSHOY: From Despotism to Revolution, 1763-1789.* *Illus.*　　　TB/3017

ALBERT GOODWIN: The French Revolution TB/1064

CARLTON J. H. HAYES: A Generation of Materialism, 1871-1900.* *Illus.*　　　TB/3039

J. H. HEXTER: Reappraisals in History: *New Views on History and Society in Early Modern Europe*　　　TB/1100

A. R. HUMPHREYS: The Augustan World: *Society, Thought, and Letters in Eighteenth Century England*　　　TB/1105

HANS KOHN, Ed.: The Mind of Modern Russia: *Historical and Political Thought of Russia's Great Age*　　　TB/1065

SIR LEWIS NAMIER: Vanished Supremacies: *Essays on European History, 1812-1918[o]*　　　TB/1088

JOHN U. NEF: Western Civilization Since the Renaissance: *Peace, War, Industry, and the Arts*　　TB/1113

FREDERICK L. NUSSBAUM: The Triumph of Science and Reason, 1660-1685.* *Illus.*　　　TB/3009

RAYMOND W. POSTGATE, Ed.: Revolution from 1789 to 1906: *Selected Documents*　　　TB/1063

PENFIELD ROBERTS: The Quest for Security, 1715-1740.* *Illus.*　　　TB/3016

PRISCILLA ROBERTSON: Revolutions of 1848: *A Social History*　　　TB/1025

ALBERT SOREL: Europe Under the Old Regime. *Translated by Francis H. Herrick*　　　TB/1121

4

N. N. SUKHANOV: The Russian Revolution, 1917:
Eyewitness Account. Edited by Joel Carmichael
Vol. I TB/1066; Vol. II TB/1067

JOHN B. WOLF: The Emergence of the Great Powers,
1685-1715.* *Illus.* TB/3010

JOHN B. WOLF: France: 1814-1919: *The Rise of a
Liberal-Democratic Society* TB/3019

Intellectual History

HERSCHEL BAKER: The Image of Man: *A Study of
the Idea of Human Dignity in Classical Antiquity, the
Middle Ages, and the Renaissance* TB/1047

J. BRONOWSKI & BRUCE MAZLISH: The Western
Intellectual Tradition: *From Leonardo to Hegel*
TB/3001

ERNST CASSIRER: The Individual and the Cosmos in
Renaissance Philosophy. *Translated with an Introduction by Mario Domandi* TB/1097

NORMAN COHN: The Pursuit of the Millennium:
*Revolutionary Messianism in medieval and Reforma-
tion Europe and its bearing on modern Leftist and
Rightist totalitarian movements* TB/1037

ARTHUR O. LOVEJOY: The Great Chain of Being: *A
Study of the History of an Idea* TB/1009

ROBERT PAYNE: Hubris: *A Study of Pride. Foreword
by Sir Herbert Read* TB/1031

BRUNO SNELL: The Discovery of the Mind: *The Greek
Origins of European Thought* TB/1018

ERNEST LEE TUVESON: Millennium and Utopia: *A
Study in the Background of the Idea of Progress.||
New Preface by the Author* TB/1134

Literature, Poetry, The Novel & Criticism

JAMES BAIRD: Ishmael: *The Art of Melville in the
Contexts of International Primitivism* TB/1023

JACQUES BARZUN: The House of Intellect TB/1051

W. J. BATE: From Classic to Romantic: *Premises of
Taste in Eighteenth Century England* TB/1036

RACHEL BESPALOFF: On the Iliad TB/2006

R. P. BLACKMUR et al.: Lectures in Criticism. *Introduction by Huntington Cairns* TB/2003

ABRAHAM CAHAN: The Rise of David Levinsky: *a
novel. Introduction by John Higham* TB/1028

ERNST R. CURTIUS: European Literature and the Latin
Middle Ages TB/2015

GEORGE ELIOT: Daniel Deronda: *a novel. Introduction
by F. R. Leavis* TB/1039

ETIENNE GILSON: Dante and Philosophy TB/1089

ALFRED HARBAGE: As They Liked It: *A Study of
Shakespeare's Moral Artistry* TB/1035

STANLEY R. HOPPER, Ed.: Spiritual Problems in Contemporary Literature§ TB/21

A. R. HUMPHREYS: The Augustan World: *Society,
Thought, and Letters in Eighteenth Century England*
TB/1105

ALDOUS HUXLEY: Antic Hay & The Gioconda Smile.*
Introduction by Martin Green TB/3503

HENRY JAMES: Roderick Hudson: *a novel. Introduction by Leon Edel* TB/1016

HENRY JAMES: The Tragic Muse: *a novel. Introduction by Leon Edel* TB/1017

ARNOLD KETTLE: An Introduction to the English
Novel. Volume I: *Defoe to George Eliot* TB/1011
Volume II: *Henry James to the Present* TB/1012

ROGER SHERMAN LOOMIS: The Development of
Arthurian Romance TB/1167

JOHN STUART MILL: On Bentham and Coleridge.
Introduction by F. R. Leavis TB/1070

PERRY MILLER & T. H. JOHNSON, Editors: The Puri-
tans: *A Sourcebook of Their Writings* Vol. I TB/1093
Vol. II TB/1094

KENNETH B. MURDOCK: Literature and Theology in
Colonial New England TB/99

SAMUEL PEPYS: The Diary of Samuel Pepys.* *Edited
by O. F. Morshead. Illus. by Ernest Shepard* TB/1007

ST.-JOHN PERSE: Seamarks TB/2002

O. E. RÖLVAAG: Giants in the Earth TB/3504

GEORGE SANTAYANA: Interpretations of Poetry and
Religion§ TB/9

C. P. SNOW: Time of Hope: *a novel* TB/1040

HEINRICH STRAUMANN: American Literature in the
Twentieth Century. *Revised Edition* TB/1168

DOROTHY VAN GHENT: The English Novel: *Form
and Function* TB/1050

E. B. WHITE: One Man's Meat. *Introduction by Walter
Blair* TB/3505

MORTON DAUWEN ZABEL, Editor: Literary Opinion
in America. Vol. I TB/3013; Vol. II TB/3014

Myth, Symbol & Folklore

JOSEPH CAMPBELL, Editor: Pagan and Christian Mys-
teries. *Illus.* TB/2013

MIRCEA ELIADE: Cosmos and History: *The Myth of
the Eternal Return§* TB/2050

C. G. JUNG & C. KERÉNYI: Essays on a Science of
Mythology: *The Myths of the Divine Child and the
Divine Maiden* TB/2014

ERWIN PANOFSKY: Studies in Iconology: *Humanistic
Themes in the Art of the Renaissance. 180 illustrations* TB/1077

JEAN SEZNEC: The Survival of the Pagan Gods: *The
Mythological Tradition and its Place in Renaissance
Humanism and Art. 108 illustrations* TB/2004

HELLMUT WILHELM: Change: *Eight Lectures on the
I Ching* TB/2019

HEINRICH ZIMMER: Myths and Symbols in Indian
Art and Civilization. *70 illustrations* TB/2005

Philosophy

HENRI BERGSON: Time and Free Will: *An Essay on
the Immediate Data of Consciousness*° TB/1021

H. J. BLACKHAM: Six Existentialist Thinkers: *Kierke-
gaard, Nietzsche, Jaspers, Marcel, Heidegger, Sartre*°
TB/1002

ERNST CASSIRER: The Individual and the Cosmos in
Renaissance Philosophy. *Translated with an Introduction by Mario Domandi* TB/1097

ERNST CASSIRER: Rousseau, Kant and Goethe. *Introduction by Peter Gay* TB/1092

FREDERICK COPLESTON: Medieval Philosophy° TB/376

RELIGION

Ancient & Classical

Biblical Thought & Literature

Judaic Thought & Literature

Christianity: Origins & Early Development

9

GEORGE SARTON: Ancient Science and Modern Civilization TB/501

HANS THIRRING: Energy for Man: *From Windmills to Nuclear Power* TB/556

WILLIAM LAW WHYTE: Essay on Atomism: *From Democritus to 1960* TB/565

A. WOLF: A History of Science, Technology and Philosophy in the 16th and 17th Centuries.° *Illus.*
Vol. I TB/508; Vol. II TB/509

A. WOLF: A History of Science, Technology, and Philosophy in the Eighteenth Century.° *Illus.*
Vol. I TB/539; Vol. II TB/540

Mathematics

H. DAVENPORT: The Higher Arithmetic: *An Introduction to the Theory of Numbers* TB/526

H. G. FORDER: Geometry: *An Introduction* TB/548

GOTTLOB FREGE: The Foundations of Arithmetic: *A Logico-Mathematical Enquiry* TB/534

S. KÖRNER: The Philosophy of Mathematics: *An Introduction* TB/547

D. E. LITTLEWOOD: Skeleton Key of Mathematics: *A Simple Account of Complex Algebraic Problems* TB/525

GEORGE E. OWEN: Fundamentals of Scientific Mathematics TB/569

WILLARD VAN ORMAN QUINE: Mathematical Logic TB/558

O. G. SUTTON: Mathematics in Action.° *Foreword by James R. Newman. Illus.* TB/518

FREDERICK WAISMANN: Introduction to Mathematical Thinking. *Foreword by Karl Menger* TB/511

Philosophy of Science

R. B. BRAITHWAITE: Scientific Explanation TB/515

J. BRONOWSKI: Science and Human Values. *Illus.* TB/505

ALBERT EINSTEIN ET AL.: Albert Einstein: Philosopher-Scientist. *Edited by Paul A. Schilpp*
Volume I TB/502
Volume II TB/503

WERNER HEISENBERG: Physics and Philosophy: *The Revolution in Modern Science* TB/549

JOHN MAYNARD KEYNES: A Treatise on Probability.° *Introduction by N. R. Hanson* TB/557

STEPHEN TOULMIN: Foresight and Understanding: *An Enquiry into the Aims of Science. Foreword by Jacques Barzun* TB/564

STEPHEN TOULMIN: The Philosophy of Science: *An Introduction* TB/513

G. J. WHITROW: The Natural Philosophy of Time° TB/563

Physics and Cosmology

DAVID BOHM: Causality and Chance in Modern Physics. *Foreword by Louis de Broglie* TB/536

P. W. BRIDGMAN: The Nature of Thermodynamics TB/537

P. W. BRIDGMAN: A Sophisticate's Primer of Relativity TB/575

A. C. CROMBIE, Ed.: Turning Point in Physics TB/535

C. V. DURELL: Readable Relativity. *Foreword by Freeman J. Dyson* TB/530

ARTHUR EDDINGTON: Space, Time and Gravitation: *An outline of the General Relativity Theory* TB/510

GEORGE GAMOW: Biography of Physics∑ TB/567

MAX JAMMER: Concepts of Force: *A Study in the Foundation of Dynamics* TB/550

MAX JAMMER: Concepts of Mass *in Classical and Modern Physics* TB/571

MAX JAMMER: Concepts of Space: *The History of Theories of Space in Physics. Foreword by Albert Einstein* TB/533

EDMUND WHITTAKER: History of the Theories of Aether and Electricity
Volume I: *The Classical Theories* TB/531
Volume II: *The Modern Theories* TB/532

G. J. WHITROW: The Structure and Evolution of the Universe: *An Introduction to Cosmology. Illus.* TB/504

A LETTER TO THE READER

Overseas, there is considerable belief that we are a country of extreme conservatism and that we cannot accommodate to social change.

Books about America in the hands of readers abroad can help change those ideas.

The U. S. Information Agency cannot, by itself, meet the vast need for books about the United States.

You can help.

Harper Torchbooks provides three packets of books on American history, economics, sociology, literature and politics to help meet the need.

To send a packet of Torchbooks [*] overseas, all you need do is send your check for $7 (which includes cost of shipping) to Harper & Row. The U. S. Information Agency will distribute the books to libraries, schools, and other centers all over the world.

I ask every American to support this program, part of a worldwide BOOKS USA campaign.

I ask you to share in the opportunity to help tell others about America.

EDWARD R. MURROW
Director,
U. S. Information Agency

[*retailing at $10.85 to $12.00]

PACKET I: Twentieth Century America

Dulles/America's Rise to World Power, 1898-1954
Cochran/The American Business System, 1900-1955
Zabel, Editor/Literary Opinion in America (two volumes)
Drucker/The New Society: *The Anatomy of Industrial Order*
Fortune Editors/America in the Sixties: *The Economy and the Society*

PACKET II: American History

Billington/The Far Western Frontier, 1830-1860
Mowry/The Era of Theodore Roosevelt and the
    Birth of Modern America, 1900-1912
Faulkner/Politics, Reform, and Expansion, 1890-1900
Cochran & Miller/The Age of Enterprise: *A Social History of
    Industrial America*
Tyler/Freedom's Ferment: *American Social History from the
    Revolution to the Civil War*

PACKET III: American History

Hansen/The Atlantic Migration, 1607-1860
Degler/Out of Our Past: *The Forces that Shaped Modern America*
Probst, Editor/The Happy Republic: *A Reader in Tocqueville's America*
Alden/The American Revolution, 1775-1783
Wright/The Cultural Life of the American Colonies, 1607-1763

*Your gift will be acknowledged directly to you by the overseas recipient.
Simply fill out the coupon, detach and mail with your check or money order.*

HARPER & ROW, PUBLISHERS • BOOKS USA DEPT.
49 East 33rd Street, New York 16, N. Y.

Packet I ☐   Packet II ☐   Packet III ☐

Please send the BOOKS USA library packet(s) indicated above, in my
name, to the area checked below. Enclosed is my remittance in the
amount of _____ for _____ packet(s) at $7.00 each.

_____ Africa   _____ Latin America

_____ Far East   _____ Near East

Name_____

Address_____

_____

NOTE: This offer expires December 31, 1966.